BOOM! **For Real**
Volume One

Edited by Steven Coy & Ian Dooda

TABLE OF CONTENTS
Poetry & Prose

TABLE OF CONTENTS
Pictures

Letter from the Editors

Dearest Reader,

This is probably the greatest anthology, ever. But the creators of the stuff within its papery walls are *entire planets* more persuasive than we, the editors—that's why we're just editors—so *please*, do not take it from us. No! Take it from the stuff inside! Yes! Stop reading this *right now* and flip through the freakin' pages already! See if something catches your eye (something surely will). Because the poems and prose and pictures herein have a whole variety of hearts—of armpit licking, bouncing mucous plugs, deliberate dismemberment, rebirthing rhubarbs, and collisions between airborne bodies, to name a few. And once you've opened and closed this dazzling new (first) edition a few times, we then recommend that you close it once more (momentarily), set it face-up on something flat, like a table-top, and just admire the thing for a few seconds silently from several steps to the side.

We thought we'd also throw in the fact that *this thing*, despite what one may think, isn't making anyone rich, at least not anytime soon. The number on the price tag (if there even is one) is nearly nothing compared to the tons of time it took to create. Nobody gets a paycheck, in other words, not even the publisher—whose name at the moment we forget how to spell—because making books independently takes bundles of money, time, love, talent, and relentless, pathetic purpose, all of which the kind contributors of this collection have in spades. Except for money.

If, after all this, you *still* aren't sold—If you somehow don't care about the crazy quantity of quality content packed in tight this tiny tome, then our best guess is you cannot read. Someone early on neglected to show you how. This is okay because *not everyone* can. Babies, for example. And slaves. Realize this doesn't make you a bad person! No! In fact, as the esteemed editors of this prominent publication, we have to admit that it's mighty impressive—if you *really* can't read—that you've managed to make it this far anyway.

Quickly Now,
Steven Coy & Ian Dooda
January 2005

In memory of Ryan Kennebeck

1982-2004

Adam Cole

Drunk at Work

"Listen up everybody," I said. The students stopped their conversations momentarily and gave me their attention. "Today's class will be a little bit different. I'm drunk."

The students looked confused and continued to stare at me as if looking for further explanation.

After I told them to get in their groups, the perplexed looks on their faces vanished and they assembled themselves accordingly. Group work. It was the wave of the future.

My students were a decent class, I supposed, compared with the other years. Well, as decent as a kindergarten class of four and five-year-olds could be. Kindergarten was a tough time for kids, and they seemed to be dealing with it alright.

Who knows why I decided to show up to work drunk today.

Last night I was at a bar having a few drinks and around 12:30 there was a power outage. So my night was cut short. I woke up and decided to make it complete by finishing off a fifth of vodka.

When I walked into class, I saw their innocent little faces and knew I wouldn't be able to lie to them. I felt pretty comfortable sharing aspects of my personal life with the kids, so I figured they deserved to know. Most of them probably had no idea what being drunk even was. I mean, sure, some of the Jewish kids probably drank wine on Shabbat and maybe even worked up a decent buzz, but that Manishewitz was nothing compared to the Russian spirits I danced with.

Not all the kids had the best grasp on life. Some just couldn't seem to keep their shit together no matter how hard they tried or what I told them. Take for instance this kid, Tommy. Nice kid. Good parents with respectable jobs. But every time I looked up, whether it was in the middle of story time or recess, the kid either had his hand down his own pants or someone else's.

"Tommy!" I'd yell. "You lose something? Quit touchin' it so much. I got one too, and you don't see me up in front of class touchin' it all the time, do you?"

Tommy would just sit there and sulk.

"Do you, Tommy? Answer me! Do you see me touching myself up in front of the class?"

"No," he'd reply, quietly.

"Thank you! That's what I thought." He usually cooperated for a good while after that. One day, though, Tommy told me, "Daddy says it's okay to touch myself." Holy shit he got me with that one. It's always a tough call when the parents get involved. I respect a father's right to parent his own kid, but it just wasn't right to go around grabbing your little pecker every five seconds and exposing it to the rest of the class every ten.

"Does your father touch himself in front of other people?" I asked Tommy. He was silent again. He was always quiet when he didn't know what to say. I knew he was young, and I didn't expect too much from the kids, but I kept grilling him for his own good. If he could learn to think quickly on his feet at an early age then he'd be pretty well off as an adult.

"Does your father touch his privates in front of other people?"

"No," replied Tommy, after hesitating for some time.

"Thank you!" Sheesh. You had to work with these kids. Teaching kindergarten wasn't as easy as it seemed. And being drunk didn't make it any easier.

When the Peace Comes

Logical steps toward
Ten people fucking in a room

Starts with huge buff arms looking as though
Constantly flexed picking up quarters one-handed

It's the back of my wrist I forgot to work on

Two unused plastic picture frames collect
The poems he wrote with his mouth
While it bit down into a sandwich with the
Corners cut off the wheat bread walls

Factories and fields and expensive machines
And angry men sitting behind desks making phone calls
Rejoice at levels equal to one another
Knowing the wheat bread has reached him safely

A teeth-gritted sigh becomes karma
For the unending war between
Body and reflected image

And not to mention

Cartoons *en español* with
Dogs barking and bleading-heart liberals
Drinking tea for energy
And flossing teeth for pleasure

Two plugs, one outlet
One ball, four squares
First recess

A child without a leg runs in fear of the whistle

New scabs for the new millennium
And mouthfuls of milk that destroy your system
Like the sound of a generator humming

Just below the level of audibility

A neighborhood jogger hears
A neighborhood dog bark
Which is a signal to the other dogs
That peace is coming soon

And the peace comes finally
Settling in by drifting down slowly to the hardwood floors
Like something light and undisturbing.

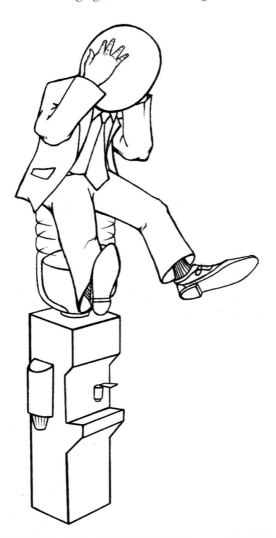

Alex Bosworth

Moths on the Moon

I remember when I was ten years old, I was sweeping up in front of our house and I couldn't help noticing how many dead moths had accumulated underneath the porch light. Dad had put in one of those 500-watt bulbs that brought in bugs from miles around. As my mother helped me scoop a pile of dried carcasses into a trash bag, I asked her:

Why are moths attracted to our porch light?

And she said:

Because they think it's the moon.

At first, I thought she was just pulling my leg or maybe some of that bug dust had gotten into her brain, so I looked it up in a book about insects and she was absolutely right.

The book said:

The instinct to follow the moon with its many varied patterns insures that the moths' population is widely disseminated.

But I thought:

What if there's more to it than that? What if it was the moths' destiny to reach the moon, but they got distracted by our stupid light bulbs? An insect's noble dream crushed because we were afraid of the dark.

Oh sure, *we* made it to the moon! We planted our little flag— did our little dance! Hell, we put the whole thing on television!

I bet there were millions of moths watching from screen doors that day in 1969, cussing us out under their breath.

"That should have been me up there!" many of them said to themselves.

And how do they wreak their vengeance on the human race? Of course, they eat our clothing when we're not looking. I happen to know that every sweater Neil Armstrong owns is riddled with holes the size of your fist. He holds them up to his wife and asks:

Honey, why do they do this?

And she says:

Maybe they think it's the moon.

façade

Andrew Bomback

Double Your Clams

Is it true that your boyfriend's father assisted on the first lung transplant, and that the man who works at the gas station next to your office won three thousand dollars on an instant lottery ticket? I really don't have much going on in my life, but it sounds as if things are working out well for you. That's not a joke. I'm serious. I miss you, but I suppose I'm happy for you, too.

I heard that you were thinking about moving to San Diego to start a catering business with your college roommates. Do you remember those nights when I would make macaroni and cheese for us, and you would sit on the couch, watching me by the stove, and smile, say things like "We should play some jazz," and then get up from the couch and play one of your Ella Fitzgerald albums on the stereo? That's not really jazz—I know, we've had this argument already—but seriously, those nights are happy memories for me.

I was watching the television yesterday—not *really* watching because the sound was off, and I was reading a magazine—but the point is that there was a commercial for soup, New England Clam Chowder, and there was a close-up shot of a can of soup, with large letters that read DOUBLE YOUR CLAMS. I came up with a funny commentary, and it would have been nice to share it with you. Although you never really thought that I was funny, did you? The times I remember you laughing were when we both were drunk, or tired, or watching movies, but never when I said something humorous.

So, San Diego, huh? The Chargers suck. The Padres, too. It's too bad you're not going to San Francisco instead. There's this song that I love—it's called "Come Back from San Francisco"—and it's this really sad love song about someone whose lover is off in San Francisco, living it up, while the singer is back in New York, alone and depressed and all the stuff of sad love songs. Anyway, I could have played that song and thought of you.

Widower

I tell people that I'm a widower, even though I've never been married and the dead wife I have in mind is actually alive and well, living somewhere in Washington State. Washougal. 473 Meridian Road. Her zip code is 98671.

We never got married in Jamaica, on a whim in the small chapel near our hotel, and we never honeymooned in Jersey City just because we wanted to be unique. We never discovered our mutual love of Flannery O'Connor's short stories in the waiting room of her oncologist, Dr. Neil O'Connor. I never tried to cheer her up by saying, "Well, think about it this way: If it weren't for the cancer, we would never have discussed *Good Country People*."

We did love each other, though. And I did try to shave every night so that when we kissed before going to sleep I didn't irritate the sensitive skin around her mouth. Even though my skin is probably just as sensitive as hers. Now that I'm a widower I can shave at a more natural frequency of once every fourth or fifth day. She always kept our refrigerator stocked with apple pie and eventually agreed with me that Billie Holiday isn't really jazz. We never went to a Grateful Dead show at Giants Stadium, certainly didn't get high in a women's bathroom stall and fuck on a broken toilet seat, but she did have a beautiful tie-dyed summer dress that always made my stomach hurt.

There's a man who plays the saxophone in my subway station. He's usually there at night when I'm returning from work, and I give him whatever change is in my pocket, sometimes a whole dollar if he's playing something I particularly like. He does this version of "God Bless America" that, I'm ashamed to admit, always gives me goose bumps. Last night he was playing "Pennies from Heaven," which my deceased wife used to sing in the shower, so I offered the man twenty dollars if he'd stop playing and have a drink with me. We went to my apartment and chased bourbon shots with grape juice. I showed him pictures and told him how lonely I was, how much I hate God for stealing my wife away, how every time I see a couple holding hands I wish death on at least one of them, sometimes both. I started to cry and asked him if he'd play "God Bless America." I took out another ten dollars from my wallet and laid it on the table. He smiled as he assembled his saxophone.

"How old are you?" he asked.

"Twenty-nine," I said.

"You're young, you'll find someone else," he said. "You've got years and years to get over her, years and years more to fall hard for another woman."

"Fitzgerald said that twenty-six is the acme of bachelorhood."

"You tell your friend Fitzgerald to go fuck himself. I'm fifty-two and I have three different girlfriends."

Anya Ezhevskaya

I Don't Speak English

I don't speak English
I don't speak English very much
Hi. How are you?
Fine, thanks.

I don't speak English
They teach me these words first
I try to write in verse
But I don't know many words
To say what I feel
But my feelings are real.

I don't speak English
But I'm learning fast to speak
Without words I am weak
Though they be strange
It's me I have to change
Because I have to tell you something so deep
it has to seep down into you
beyond words
that's why it hurts
So much. Because...

I don't speak English.
They taught me these words first
If I spoke better I would have told them
that reverse psychology doesn't work
very well in this case and if you want a kid to learn English
then "I don't speak English" is *not* the best way to start.

But I couldn't say it then
And even now I doubt if anybody understands
Really, from the soul, from the heart
From the place where words fall apart

Either into definitions or meaning
A feeling which
Rather than concealing
Reveals.

What one wants to say.
But not today.
You see.

I don't speak English.
Though I've become quite versatile with
Translation
Configuration of macromolecular peptides
Transfigurations of letters bonded together
into words.

But what hurts more than anything
Is that, though I can make the sounds,
I don't really feel English through and through
The way you do
Without even knowing it.

My friend, you'd only know it if you too were
A stranger in a strange land
Where suddenly you find
You can't express quite what you mean,
Just dance around it.
I hope you understand,
My friend,
Because
I don't speak English.

But if I did, I'd tell you:

Я так тебя люблю.

Beau Gunderson

Dr. J

It's Sunday and I've just woken up and my sacrilegious toast is waiting for me in the toaster. It's got Jesus on one side and Satan on the other; they're both wearing tennis shorts and holding rackets. Jesus is shown mid-serve. He's got a sweatband on and it fits perfectly on his head. Satan is shown leaning on his racket and smoking an Old Gold. He's got red skin and yellow eyes and he looks pretty ripped. He's wearing a sweatband too. It's stained.

I bought this bread at the dollar-store on the waterfront, mainly because I'd never seen a dollar-store sell bread before. Especially not incredibly detailed bread with religious figures as tennis players embossed in each slice. I bought out the entire stock and put them all in my freezer. I make sandwiches with it every day, but on Sundays I like to eat it for breakfast with scrambled eggs.

I roll up a red bandana with a silhouette of Julius Erving in the center and wrap it around my head. Me and Dr. J head outside to garden while it's still warm. I grow nothing but daisies here. I take a picture of them every day so that the world will be able to see daisies grow and die before their eyes.

I like Daisy but no one else does. I've watched her grow and die in the eyes of others. They angered with her because they changed while she did not. They tired of borrowing her way of looking at things and gave it back. They pretended to her that it was theirs all along. It won them nothing.

I haven't talked to my parents in a while. It's probably time to tell them what I've been up to. There's a blank sheet of paper thumb-tacked to the wall. I bang my head against it until there's some blood on it to sign my name.

On my way to the post office, two men accost me and ask if I've spoken to Jesus recently. I tell them I ate him for breakfast.

Blake Butler

Born Inside a Watermelon

Everything is pink and cold at his first sight, an unchanging landscape. The baby's grown into consciousness not in a womb, but with the outline of his body surrounded by the sweet, crisp flesh of the melon, inside the rind. He wails a breath and has his mouth filled with the semi-soft gunk, spreading out along the inside of his lips to fill his cheeks. He swallows and feels the food-bubble descend through his esophagus, to be dissolved in stomach acid.

Despite the opacity of the rind, everything inside the fruit is aglow. He can see his tiny fingers, his curving legs, the many black seeds that might one day become other fruits impregnated with things like him. He's full of wait.

Occasional thumps disrupt the quiet of the fruit, thick resounding bursts of sound that even from inside he knows are the quality-checking finger taps of customers examining his melon for purchase. Most likely, he thinks, they don't know he's in there. He's hopeful, though. He waits to be discovered, to be taken home and sliced free, lifted from the wet margin of the melon and put into diapers, into a crib, to eventually one day grow into a man. He promises himself that if all of this is allowed to happen, he will make the most of every moment.

He's growing older. He begins to realize that his body is swelling, maturing into a size that will soon be too large to be contained within the fruit. He's been careful over time to eat only enough to make room for expansion but now, as his backbone presses into the soft white inside, he knows he'll soon grow too large, and the median will burst. And if not that, then the decay will catch up, eating away the melon over time into something indigestible, something gross. To save space he crunches down as tightly as he can, with his knees against his chest and head tucked in, afraid of what waits outside.

It's not long until the insides are all black, just as he's feared, decked with strings of splotchy brown as the melon rots. The smell is still sugary but split with an undercurrent of ruin, the promise that change is near. He imagines standing outside his melon and measuring it with his hands, seeing the once green luster of the outside now withered and white, impossible to want, perhaps revolting. The thought saddens him.

With his weight, he knocks back and forth to make the melon roll over and spin. Doing so makes him dizzy at first, nauseous, but he holds tight, rolls into the nausea. Going in and over himself inside the melon he knows he couldn't have far to roll before something happens. He anticipates the impact, ready for the rind that owns him to splatter and desist, and for whatever else may come to come.

Bob Surrat

Asshole

Gentrification is a dirty word where I come from
I wish they would have just left Golden Hills alone
It's like you've got to have a fucking college degree just to afford
    the means of this once working-class neighborhood

Educations are like assholes
and mine farts when I drop knowledge
I guess that makes my two cents not worth what it once was,
just enough to talk the coffee shop chick out of another cup

Educations are like assholes
and mine spatters when I drink their diuretics
Where I come from, it's a sad day when the 99-cent store
    becomes an art gallery
and the local drunk bar becomes a steak and supper club for all
the flaming hipster cowboys
that made this place so popular

Tattoos are like assholes
and the ink on mine that reads "exit only" is beginning to run
I'm going to take a shit in a paper bag
I'm going to leave it on their porch and light it on fire

Now, don't get me wrong
It's not that I hate all transplants
If not for transplants,
I might have never received that new heart
of which I was in such need

It's just that I get so upset that death has to occur
in order for organ donations to happen at all

My wrists bleed
and the crown of thorns that I once wore

when I was king of the hill
pricks my index finger with which I write
    the graffiti of the locals
The crime spree I've been planning is the only thing that keeps
    us hopeful—
the only thing that we have to keep these fucking slumlords
    in check
I've been trying to get one rolling for years
I think it's time for at least one more attempt

Apartments are like assholes
I think I'll go find one that's cheaper
Cause just because these whores got some new clothes
don't mean that we ain't had 'em before
It's those same vaginal walls that have pencil markings
recording how tall little Bobby was
first at three feet, then four, and so on
till eventually I was too old for that sentimental bullshit

Now look at me
getting all emotional
trying to hang on to a neighborhood
    that has finally outgrown me
Cause I don't have a cowboy hat or any tattoos
or an education
I'm just another asshole

Cheryl Tupper

Ode to a '64 T-Bird

The truth
Of your bone-white steering wheel
Sliding through my hands

Perfection
of sag in the driver's seat
Which knows my butt well

I am bad
Illuminated
In the green-radon glow
Of your still-gleaming dash

Bad
Behind your chromework
Behind the vast expanse of your hood

And under the hood
Oh, mechanic's delight!
Your V8 4-barrel
Luxuriously sprawled
A mystery to me
And to photocopied imports
Left confused in your wake

But the Bird replies
Truth is beauty
Beauty, truth
That is all ye need to know

"Cruise on."

Darby Larson

My Friend Olo

My friend Olo can shove an entire Rubik's cube into his mouth and solve it with his tongue. His real name is Oleander.

The reason Olo has this uncanny ability, or at least the reason he can get the thing into his mouth, is his open lips form a perfect square. It's some sort of physiological anomaly. He doesn't really need to force the cube into his mouth. It just kind of slips in like a block peg. Still, how he is able to see the colors while it's in his mouth is a mystery to me.

It must be that he studies it like crazy just before he inserts it, and then, having memorized the exact sequences needed for solving, executes the required tongue thrusts accordingly. His face is the strangest thing to look at while he's solving it. Like he's trying to chew an entire apple at once.

And sure enough, he spits the thing out and there it is: orange, blue, red, green, yellow, white. Nice and pretty.

"Olo," I say, "Olo, how in the hell did you learn to do this?"

"Practice," he says, "practice."

"Also, Olo, why did your parents name you 'Oleander'? Isn't that a girl's name?"

"You're one to talk, Darby."

We walk down the street together: Olo, with a cubish bulge in his pants, threatening to rip the seam, and I, debating whether or not to give him a pat on the back.

David Barringer

Our Records Show

Our records show that you recently purchased our Women's Cashmere Baby Sling (BS 45). This baby sling may not contain cashmere as advertised. The garment was intended to be a blend of new wool, nylon, and .05% cashmere. Subsequent testing revealed inconsistencies in the fabric too late for us to edit catalog copy. While the baby sling remains a warm and classic style, free of pending product-liability suits, we will understand if you do not want to use it as a baby sling. We recommend that you store onions in it. Use it as a dog sweater. Yes, try that. A dog sweater.

Our records show that you visit a foot reflexologist. Stop it.

Our records show that you had sunstroke this summer. Are you okay?

Our records show that you never learned to drive a tractor. Your grandfather drove a tractor when he was eight years old. Your great-grandfather was not a farmer but he did own a Model T and made a living painting the homes of employees of the Ford Motor Company at a time when Henry Ford was busy changing the American way of life. Another great-grandfather was the president of a carpenters' union in Illinois. What the hell are you doing?

Our records show that you are afraid of growing old. This is common.

Our records show that art and entertainment depicting suffering in the world may simply add to the suffering in the world. We are confused.

Our records show that child prodigies love dogs but are never allowed to own them. As a result, these child prodigies learn never to trust authority. We think this is unfair to authority.

Our records show that the hedonist is at work. What gives?

Our records show that the narcissist is in therapy. It's probably a ruse.

Our records show that you are not a notorious lollygag from an occupied territory. You are lucky.

Our records show that your least favorite smell is "the smell of pity." What are you, a smart-ass?

Our records show that seriousness is heavier than trouble. We recommend trouble on long walks through the desert of a monogamous relationship. And wineskins. Two or three wineskins.

Our records show that no one owns the spaces between the stars. We can't believe this. Who do we talk to?

Our records show that your friend is recovering and while it may take a while, she plans on forgiving you. You didn't hear it from us.

Our records show that you are not doing anything Saturday night. We know an osteopath on the Lower East Side. You like manicotti?

Our records show that someone has a really big bomb. Have you heard this too?

Our records show that you had a dream about a man who walked in place. Every time he took a step, the whole world was rebuilt a little bit ahead of him so that when he put his foot down he was putting it down in the same place, relatively speaking, that he started from. He never got anywhere. Think of how much work would have to be done to make this happen. It is impossible that everyone in the world would care about that man so much they would work that hard just to make that man's life easier. Greedy people work very hard making movies about handsome people for boring people to watch. Go see one.

Our records show that you believe natural disasters are "bad" even though they are "natural." Did you go to college?

Our records show you are considering opening a bed and breakfast in Kashmir as soon as both sides decide to "stop fighting" and "share." Accounting thinks you're bluffing.

Our records show that they never interview anyone in the audience funnier than the host. You know when someone in the audience tries to be funnier than the host? You kind of feel embarrassed for the guy because he doesn't seem to understand the dynamics of the show. It's kind of sad, and people roll their eyes, and sometimes viewers change the channel. Advertisers don't like it. They pull their ads out, take their money to some other show where the morons in the audience keep their mouths shut and play along and don't try to ruin it for everybody else. You got that, amigo?

Our records show that someone named "Fellen Brooke Monet" writes us angry letters. We believe this is a made-up name. Do you send angry letters to us?

Our records show an increase in on-demand consumer laboratory testing for health screening. What have you been telling people?

Our records show that you are planning to write a story called, "Frequent Sucker Points and Other Failures in Marketing." We have enclosed a gift certificate in the amount of $10 to dissuade you from ending your career on such a pathetic note.

Our records show all balls in play.

Our records show that it is no news to us that our records must be interpreted before they "show" anything. Not to mention that our records are merely our "records," as well as only nominally "our" records. Let it go.

Our records show you have crafted a personal morality. This morality provides incentives for you to overcome your fears and realize your dreams. This morality grew out of an unflinching assessment of what currently goes on in America. This assessment might be illegal. Send us a copy.

Our records show that a TV executive is pitching a new reality program titled "The People Show." Is this guy a moron or what? Would you watch a program like this? Would you rather watch it at 8 pm or 10 pm? How much money do you make a year?

Our records show that we have made little effort to come to a conclusion about the ethical issues surrounding stem-cell research. To be honest, we are more worried about hybrid insect robots escaping research labs, even though we don't know what we'd do about them if they did get loose. Still, we can't stop thinking about them. Hybrid insect robots. Jesus.

Our records show that mortals can always try again. Up to a point. And then they can't.

David Gianatasio

You Want a Piece of Me?

I'd say she was 18, maybe younger, slumped against the yellow-ing, filth-caked tiles of the winding tunnel leading up from the subway platform to the street. "He took... he took..." That's all she could say. Her cheeks were stained with tears, her dark hair sweat-streaked and strangely twisted, as if someone had grabbed a hand-ful, yanking until the strands were uprooted from the scalp. She'd been mugged, no doubt about it, though I hadn't actually witnessed the crime. A purple welt bloomed on one cheek and she shivered despite the oppressive humidity that seemed worse here in the tun-nel, stale air wafting down from the graffiti-soaked ceiling above. It took her a few minutes to notice me; when she did, she regarded me strangely, fear, uncertainty and hope flashing in her eyes. The time had come. I knelt beside her and gripped my left wrist with my right hand, firmly but gently, twisting slowly, working the joint with an even, measured pressure until, with a soft pop and mini-mal discomfort, the hand detached. A clean break. Bloodless. She stared up at me open-mouthed but, unlike some, she didn't scream or faint. She accepted my gift and I smiled. "It's a strong hand," I said. "It's served me well in more than a few fights. But it can also be a comforting hand." Her sobbing ceased as I moved on into the crowd below.

I met up with the mugger as I exited the train seven stops down the line. (It was the kind of coincidence you could never get away with in fiction. Actually, my luck always runs that way.) He was younger than his victim, 15 or 16—with a hard face and darting eyes more suited to a homeless 'Nam vet than a teenager decked out in designer jeans and an aviator jacket that probably cost more than I pay each month in rent. There was no one else around. Our eyes locked and a strange look crossed his face. He could sense that I knew what he'd done, or else he had another mugging in mind. His hand slid inside his waistband. Was he feeling around for a knife or a razor blade? It didn't matter. I stepped back a few paces and, balancing somewhat awkwardly on my right leg, wrenched my left foot from its socket. (I did this quickly, in one sharp motion, causing myself quite a bit of pain, because I was afraid he'd bolt and I was in no mood to chase him down, what with the heatwave so unbearable and all.) Flesh and bone dripped from the stump, but I was confident the healing process would begin before the first trickle of blood hit the ground. (My limbs always begin to grow back immediately; that's just how it works. And if any people happen to be around, well, they just don't seem to notice what's going on. It's like me and the person I'm "gifting" are inhabiting our own, private universe. That's how it works. Don't ask my why.) Anyway, the kid was in shock, stiff as a statue; a six-inch shiv slid from his fingers, clattered onto the tracks. As I hobbled away, I nodded back to where the foot stood, still shod in imitation suede, like a work of abstract art. I shrugged. "Maybe you can use it next time, to help you outrun the cops." The kid was barely breathing. "And there's a twenty in the sock. That's what you wanted—money? Right?"

I should've had more patience with Cliff. He's been a great neighbor and friend. We've shared the little things that in some ways are the most important. He's always available to split a pizza or let me come by and watch pay-per-view. Sometimes, we chat until the early morning hours. He's been going through a rough time lately, but I was just too distracted to really focus on what he had to say. My foot hadn't finished growing back and the throbbing was driving me mad. My hand itched too; always does afterward, but this time it was really bad. I was scratching off the freshly regenerated skin. Cliff just rambled on. "She's playin' me… playin' with my head, right? Her lawyer called three times yesterday, three freakin' times… at my *job*. I'm gonna be out on my ass. And she's gonna get the kids—she's already turning them against me. What should I do? What would *you* do?" I sighed deeply; indeed, there was only one thing I *could* do. I began working on an eyeball. Sure, Cliff's problems didn't have anything to do with vision or sight in the literal sense. Even so, my gifts operate on more of a spiritual and metaphysical (not to mention, metaphorical) level. My eye would help Cliff see things clearly; I had no doubt of that.

A week later, I could barely lift my head. My hand itched worse than poison ivy and the flesh was red and blistered. My toes had grown back all wrong; the damn foot looked like a hoof and it was hurting more by the minute, sending waves of fire up and down my spine. My eye returned gray and filmy, sightless, along with a headache that drove spikes deep inside my brain. I was splayed out on the sofa when Cliff came by, using the spare key I'd given him in case of emergencies. I struggled to rise from the pillows, but couldn't quite make it. Cliff had an earnest look on his face and again he rambled on. I could only make out about every third word, and even those came through distorted and vague.

I thought I heard him say something about a *heart*... his heart going out to me, or else he had a broken heart, something like that... as he smiled and lifted his hands. Then he cracked his knuckles and flexed his fingers, leaning in close as he reached for the buttons of his shirt.

Or was he reaching out for mine?

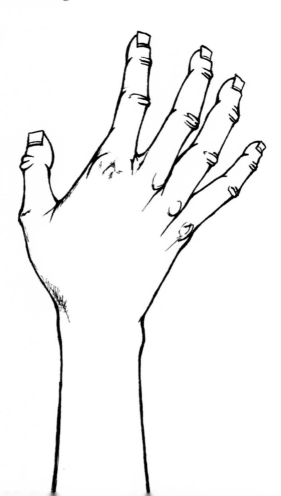

Dennis Mahagin

When The Buzzards Shout "No Ac!" You Are On Thin Ice

Mike Tyson's peripatetic
pet bengal tiger
pacing the open faced
block-long excavation crypt
in Parumph, Nevada

where a middle aged
casino mogul
with a checkered past
buried twenty tons
of silver bullion

nine months before
the post-adolescent
psychopathic newlywed wife
clamped his ripcord neck
between her tender thighs
and squeezed
a half-pint of heroin
into his twitching esophagus
with a turkey baster.

All this stuff is true—
the glare
of the sun,
the satiated tiger's
unrepentant yawn,

and those endless
striations
of heat coming off
the desert floor
like stretch marks
on a forty-year-old hooker

bending over backwards
to get you off.

It's all true—even that
Howard Hughes poltergeist
over by the windmill

tapping the ash
off a Camel
non-filter

right into the humidor ribcage
of a tourist from Cleveland
sporting a ten inch slit
above the right hip

where they sucked out his liver
and Fed Exed it
to Evil Knievel's ranch
in Bozeman, Montana—

that's right, go ahead
and pop my frying eyes out
with a cantaloupe scoop
if I'm lying

but here it is
already

a hundred
and eight degrees
at round noon
in an alley behind
the Boulevard Mall
and something dred-locked
and spectral

—hardly human at all—

sucks a cluster of glass splinters
from the busted crack vial
embedded
in a bleeding palm,

trying to get that taste
into the back of his throat

one more time

the tiger
throws back its head,
roaring at the irradiated sky

and somewhere
in southeastern Alaska
a glacier slaps itself
on the thigh,

thunderclap-cackling
as yet another hundred-ton
skein of baby-blue ice
goes sloughing off
into the sea.

Doug Tanoury

Ode To Feet

I have seen poetic feet so perfect,
The very smallest units
Of patterned stress,
Soft idioms of Iambic
And drum beats of Anapestic,
That march across the carpet
In measured meter toward full-length mirrors.

I am the bard of bare soles
And naked ankles,
Of fallen arches and
Swollen heels,
Of toenails
Pedicured and painted,
That catch the light
Like so many cut sapphires,
All arranged
In descending order of size.

I have crafted couplets in Trochaic,
And started the heartbeat of lines in Spondaic,
For I am the poet of feet,
Perfect and imperfect,
Poetic
And otherwise,
Of bunions, bumps, and bent toes,
Carried within or laid upon
A pump, mule, sandal, or thong.

Retail Egyptology

In the supermarket
Where navel oranges are stacked high
With monumental precision
Like the great pyramid of Giza,
And Santa Rosa plums
Form a lesser monument
For a more mediocre monarch
In The Valley of the Kings.

I am the jackal-faced god,
A duster of old bones
And petrified flesh,
Who breathes the desert air
At 5:00 a.m. and peers wearily
Over the meat counter
For a fleeting glimpse
Of the floating head
Of Queen Nefertiti
In hopes her regal gaze
Will fall on my English cut roast.

Awake, Osiris, to the sound
Of the Nile's water
And sea birds calling from the reeds
To catch the gleam of light
On stainless steel countertops
For it is the deli meats
Hanging in long strands from the ceiling,
Indeed it is the garlic bologna and hard salami
That unites the upper and lower kingdoms.

Duane Locke

Only The Dead

You, as beautiful as petrified wood,
My woman without motion,
My dead woman;

But you are living, and remain
As beautiful as the sound of an oboe
Played at twilight by a river.

My dead woman,
You carry scissors in your pockets,
Scissors to cut away the flicker of sun spots on water.

My living woman, you run in front of cedars,
Your body is curved
Like the paths butterflies make in the air.

An orchestra in white plays black waltzes,
As you sleep underground, my dead woman.
Living, you passionately rub your fingertips
Over a bleached shell you do not hold.

I don't want you dead, for I want
The blood in your heart to ring like glass bells.
I don't want you dead, for I want you
To take off your clothes, be as naked as white wine.

You are alive, but I can't have you
When you are alive,

It is the way of the world, no presence,
I can only have you when you are dead.

Scholars, Stains, and Salvation

Scholars in black raincoats stroll in ovals,
Trying to decide
If it were garlic or morning glories
That with a *coup d'état* founded a Balkan government,
Never noticing it is not raining,
But knowing the idea of rain
Is more real than rain,
So each scholar in dry weather
Is sprinkled with rain drops.

Today is misty,
Only the eyes of the white oxen are seen
As three oxen stand between Cottonwoods.

Fog clarifies the foolish world
Invented by our wisdom,
Different from scholars,
I seek stains.
I search piazzas for stained
Persephones and Proserpines.
Goddesses, bodies in marble
Are always naked,
And the stains are
A dark orange cape
Spread across a shoulder,
The orange cape
Put there by inclement weather.
These patinas
Added by rain
Or the idea of rain
By time, or an idea of time
Are orange, a unique orange,
Not similar to any other orange
On our earth, and serve as a guide to salvation.

The Hague

The Hague grew out of light,
The seed,
A star buried in the earth.
It is a crystal transparent cloth
Washed on stones
By the wind's hands,
The dust particles on the brooms
Have halos.
In the windows, large,
Never opaque,
The light is transparent lace.
The moon never departs
But stays all day in flower pots.
The avenues leisurely stroll,
Lovingly holding the canals, hands.
All the houses
Are Vermeer paintings
Hung on the sky.

Ian Thal

Beacon Hill Panorama with Paper Airplanes

Paper airplanes glide over
spire-pierced green oxidized copper showing through
tar-covered skylight bubbled slanting roofs
where under octogonal cupola blisters
persian cats prowl lazily about trellised gardens
eyeing television antennae where sparrow hawks roost.

Paper airplanes trace arcs
dragging eyes over the Longfellow Bridge
as it sends red and white 01700s to and fro
a Cambridge cityscape sunset silhouetted
under mammoth crane-hoisting scaffolds
and then towards the *three hundred sixty-four point four* smoot
and one ear length of Mass Ave Bridge
spanning the Charles meander meander waters
and past the defunct Citgo sign still flashing
marking Kenmore Square under a Venusian firmament pin-prick.

Another hand-folded craft's flight path curves
under a moon rising over the federal reserve
luminating pink the gold leafed Statehouse dome
while an elevated green-line track
glanced through apertures
between Beacon Hill brownstones
sends trolleys to Science Park and Lechmere.

Folded paper in flight
the blue-lit white suspension cables
of the Zakim Bridge radiate like fish fins
while the Tobin points to Salem
and points unseen.

And paper airplanes spiral for blocks
falling through the leafy capturing canopy
that bursts between brick buildings
gliding over Russell and
catching Irving Street updrafts
landing by lawn chairs and picnic tables
on Beacon Hill rooftops.

Jackie Corley

The Suburban Swindle

God cut through somebody's soul and spread his hands across the clouds. It hovers there, that swollen wound in the sky, the skin stretched thin and pursing at the gash. The grass is soft and clean and thick and we don't touch the dirt—the kid and me—when we lie down to see. I ease up on my elbow. I slide one finger under his bangs and one above and rub the smooth valley along the bridge of his nose with my thumb. He needs a trim soon, I remind myself.

"What do you think, buddy?"

He shrugs his shoulders quickly, deliberately indifferent—like anything else would exhaust his patience or gratify mine. He's a moth beating out the color of his wings. I move my hand to the roundness of his cheek, feel it warm in my palm. It'll start squaring off in a year or two. Another reminder but less benign, this one. He swats my hand away and I smile.

"All right, all right." I fall back onto this soft, groomed football field we've commandeered and link my fingers behind my head. "How's school?"

Another swift shrug—I hear it muffled in the grass.

I flick my chin toward the sky. "Looks bloody, doesn't it?"

"It looks like your big fat butt," he says, smacking my side with the back of his hand.

"Oh yeah?" I sit up, tap my fists along his belly and baby-flesh ribs. "Oh yeah?" He laughs from some place primal—this deep, guttural laugh. He's nowhere else right now.

The mother had me come up from school this weekend. Something with the father. He got his charge off a bottle of WinterMint Listerine and the kid found him in the backyard, in the darkness, stripped to his shorts and dancing. At least he wasn't jerking off into those new bushes you guys got, I tell her. She doesn't laugh. She doesn't hear me. She just keeps chirping through this electric wire that tethers me back there.

I've got this numbness in my head, these blind eyes. When I was ten I'd get home from school and play Mario Kart for hours, just me in the basement. I'd never remember advancing through the races, though. It'd be coming on dinner and I'd keep a straight spine in the early winter darkness. I'd snap awake to my mother's voice at the top of the steps. That's how I drive this sterile turnpike now—with a slack, watery consciousness. I know the highways on instinct. Always one game or another, I guess.

The kid's not like I was at his age. I pull up to the house at 5 o'clock and he's with his wolf pack playing baseball on a neighbor's front yard. He's the youngest of them, so his shoulders are always puffed up to his neck—a stiff bow drawn round, like he's ready for a fight. I lean against the car, watching him and debating on another cigarette. I keep my distance. Whenever I hear them picking on him, I want to run over and light their hairless nuts on fire. He has an image to protect, though, so I stay away. All these quiet traces in the sand between him and me.

When he finally comes to me, he's screwing around with his walk—pounding the concrete, one hopping basketball sneaker at a time, throwing his arms around in waves. He freezes in front of me with a guppy-mouth and leering, laughing eyes, pretending to be fascinated.

"You turd." I grin, pushing his head to the side.

"Did you hear about Dad?"

"Yeah, I heard about Dad."

I wrap a firm hand around the back of the kid's neck and start moving him up the driveway.

"You're gonna move, aren't you? You're gonna move, you little girl!" I keep my bones warped hard to the rubber grip of the handlebars, my ass hovering above the seat of my bike. We're racing the track around the football field in opposite directions. Whoever veers out of the other's way loses. It's usually me—I usually move first.

I keep my eyes on him and as we close the gap at the last straightaway, he boils into the horizon. My mind goes blank. I get the cool rush, that sweeping blackness when you stand up too fast. And I'm faking sameness and hoping it goes away before I lose my balance. The world fizzles back through TV snow and suddenly that beautiful, blue-eyed baby is right there in front of me with his fear balled up in a tight scream and a wide, white face.

I plow into his back wheel and we both fall square on our tailbones. He's shouting at me as I untangle us from the bikes.

"What's wrong with you?" he says. "Why did you do that, stupid? I hate you!" He punches me hard but goes for my bicep, like he's unsure. He hesitates and hits me there again but softer this time. "I hate you!" he growls.

And what I do, what I do is start bawling. I pull him to my body—this shaking, wet mess of me. "I'm an asshole. I'm so sorry. I love you so much, buddy. I love you so much." But it's all wrong.

I want to tell him something. When I was your age, kid, your uncle tried to cut through to his heart. He didn't make it, but he spilt all his holy breath. I want to tell him something like that, make it thick and beautiful. But it wasn't. The uncle had a dustless, frozen room and he was just a clean body in his first full suit, swaying at the end of a length of rope. It broke me when I was the kid's age, when the uncle had the 21 years I have now.

I'm still holding the kid, rocking him. He lets me.

I press my lips to the sharp strands of hair starting to crawl over the top of his ear. "We're split twins, you and me," I whisper. He has that damp, sour boy-sweat smell that I hate. I don't want him to become a young man, all that quiet violence and sadness building up to something solid and bitter inside of him. I fear it. I fear losing him.

Yes, split twins. Split by time. Ancient wars, words, emptiness, factions, fractions, seconds. Ten years separate us. He's more than me for basting that long.

"When do you have to go back?" the kid asks. He's got those bright eyes on me in that face of his that's really my face.

He's on the sidewalk and I'm walking in the grass next to him, pushing my bike on the street close to the curb. I nudge the kid's shoulder with two bent fingers. "What? You want me to leave, douche? Huh?" I tickle his neck and he clamps my hand between the heel of his jaw and his collarbone. "Huh?"

"No," he says. "I don't like being alone with them."

"I know. I know you don't."

"You're lucky you don't have to stay."

"I know, buddy."

We walk quietly for a couple minutes. Pebbles and dirty glass scratch the gravel under my wheel. The kid kicks fresh white puffs of dandelions across pretty green lawns—his little contribution to the suburban swindle.

Life made this thing practical for me. I have these conversations back at school all detached and ironic and logical. School and money and the future. My own life, my own family someday. But there's this darkness in me because I'm glad I don't have to stay.

I can't tell the college kids that. I can't give them any substance, I can't frame this thing for them. What I can do, what I can do for me, I can run roughshod through my past and connect the dots with all the broken boys I've seen crawl. The bored, drippy-eyed potheads in basements, anesthetizing their gods' minds. The drunk fighters, cut through and burning, licking livewire wounds and then pretending they're numb. The walking egos, all assholes for mouths, holding cigarettes for Goth chicks and whores, for users who'll fuck them. Or minor men like the uncle, who walk through life straight, and then kill themselves when they turn invisible.

Some of those broken boys get lucky, some of them find girls with soft hands to stroke their heads and kiss their eyes and whisper and keep them cool. They quit hiding and let the break settle wide and still inside them. Those boys let themselves get saved for an hour or two.

I even had myself one of those boys once. It happened when I was so steady and thick like bricks and molding that I didn't know the whole wall could get pushed down. I cut these fierce teeth on the world—no one could touch me. I was rolling anger in black T-shirts and sneakers and baggy jeans, fists balled up and tensed at my sides as I walked alone down a hall. There wasn't going to be another uncle, not out of me. Nobody was going to win anything off me.

Then I found my boy. He was a heavy iron chest, but for some reason he showed me his wounds. I told him I could heal him. I told him when the wind blew it was me sweeping up around him. I told him a lot of things I thought I could do, like I was more than human, or greater than Guinness, at least. And I didn't see it at the time, but I got kneaded soft inside just saying those things. But one day the clock stopped on us and we saw that all I'd built up was voodoo and shadows. So that iron chest slammed shut and he graduated to Jack Daniels and bumps of coke to cast a better spell.

I'm scared for the kid, for where and when the knife falls. That day'll come when he'll see through me, when I'm just the limp, boring sister chewing filters out of her cigarettes. He'll see I can't save him, that there's nothing in me that could save anybody. Mostly

I'm scared the kid'll wind up just some other fool and snarl and run from any naïve thing who thinks she can hold him.

I wonder how much he knows, how much I can tell him and make him understand. The kid is rolling his bike wheel over the head of a dead, sun-dried garden snake lying on the sidewalk.

"You can't hurt it," I say. "It's dead."

The kid doesn't look up at me. He keeps methodically pressing his tire down onto the crackling corpse. I grab the metal frame of the bike just above the tire and pull it back, then I bend at the waist, one leg in the air for balance. I take the flat snake and toss it into the center of a lawn. The kid looks up at me with his top lip pressed thin against the bottom. He is confused and I don't know how to tell him that I don't have an answer. I've seen boys with wide eyes breaking, but not this one, not my eyes in a boy like that, my brother.

48

Code Name: Betty Crocker

Godzilla is stumbling through Belgrade.

An air-raid siren winds up as the bombs start falling again: boom of monster footsteps.

I'm so thirsty I've been sipping a pint of vodka. It's making things worse. Earlier, I was arguing with my mother. How she found me hiding in an executive suite beneath the bombed Chinese embassy I don't know.

I'm wearing a Viking helmet with plastic horns and a red superhero's cape. Prior to the cruise missile strike there was a Chinese party. Now it's dark.

"There is a microwave in here," a voice is saying. "I know it's here. I saw it. Where is it?"

I open my eyes but can't see anything. "It's in the kitchen, Mom," I call. "Next to the fridge."

I am grabbed by my cape and now I can see a face close to mine—pointed, unshaven, bad breath—demanding: "Who are you?"

"I'm a war correspondent."

He stares. Then: "A journalist." He spits, "A liar."

"I wouldn't quite put it that way, man. I dropped out of school to come over here."

"School? University?"

I nod.

"You're a fool, then."

"I've been stringing for the AP, man. My stuff's been in the Times."

"Gah!" He tosses me back on the couch. "There was a microwave oven in this apartment," he says. "I saw it during a meeting. Where is it?"

"In the kitchen, man. Like I said."

The thin outline of his body becomes clear. A Yugoslav soldier. The onion smell of body odor is overpowering. He disappears into the kitchen and then returns carrying the big box of microwave. It's an Eighties model: huge, with a dial. He plants it in my lap.

"Carry this," he says. "Go."

I step on the power cord and nearly trip myself as I stand.

"Be careful," he hisses.

"It's just a fucking microwave, dude."

I feel the cold touch of what I assume to be a pistol muzzle against my cheek.

"Move," he says.

I lead the way upstairs and through a bent metal door into the damp midnight outside. All the buildings are dark. The air smells like burnt plastic. He directs me: *Down this street. Go there. Turn.* The streets are wet. My red cape snaps in the wind.

Then he's muttering: "We have a Soviet SA-2—surface-to-air missile. Air Defense System. We'll use the microwaves to trick NATO anti-radiation missiles, then fire on their bombers. Their bombers are slow."

I'm struggling with the bulky tin box. "Microwaves. You're kidding me. How many microwaves?"

"Many. As many as we can get. We will deploy them all throughout the city."

"You're in charge of microwave oven deployment? How the hell is a microwave going to divert a bomb?"

"Same type of radio frequency as the SA-2 radar. The bombs fall on parachutes until the seeker head tracks RF, then they let go and fall to target."

I blink. "You just set the timer, leave the door open and go? Power on high?"

"Yes. Yes."

"That's wild, man. That's like Anarchist's Cookbook stuff. Betty Crocker's recipe for bomb-diversion. Microwave ovens everywhere, pointed at the sky."

I stumble on a brick and he shoots me a grimace. I tighten my grip on the box. We're going deeper into the toppled city. The terrain of World War II documentaries. The cityscape is like broken teeth.

Then his girlfriend, Margo, joins us. She's a masseuse. She says she likes touching people. She asks if my shoulders are sore.

"Yes."

When she asks what I'm doing here, her boyfriend sneers: "He's not writing about the war, anymore. He's part of the action." He waves his pistol at me. "Isn't that what journalists always want?"

"I'm carrying the microwave," I say. "That's what I'm doing here."

"Don't listen to him," Margo tells me. "A journalist for the state newspaper wrote an article about his father, and Milosevic had him murdered."

She touches the soldier's cheek and his hard face softens. "If we could all simply touch each other, there would be no bombs," Margo says wistfully. Then she glances at me, asking: "My being here changes the entire tone of your article, doesn't it?"

Before I can respond there is a whistle: a short high scream in the air that strikes so suddenly we can't even move. I hear him say "Cruise Missile," and then the sky is white. A wave of concussion shocks through us, and when I open my eyes I am lying in the street, ear on the wet concrete. The microwave lies smashed not far away. I take my hand away from my ear and see the wetness is blood.

"You'll be fine," Margo is saying. I can barely hear her. We're sitting on the curb. Everything seems distant. She's drying my ear with the dirty hem of my cape.

"The poet hallucinates by firelight while the cities burn," I say.

"You're in shock." She nods toward a pair of boots jutting from underneath a collapsed concrete wall, Wicked Witch-style. Margo holds up a GPS receiver and then puts a finger on my slack lips.

"Special Forces," she explains, smiling. "They can't divert Tomahawks."

She takes my reporter's notebook, saying "I'll need this," and adjusts the Viking helmet on my head. I look around like a toddler, head bobbing. Dawn is glowing beyond the smashed buildings.

Margo's eyes are deep brown. She is still smiling as she stands, executes a slight skip, and kicks me in the face.

Jamie Allen

The First Catapult

In the neighboring village of Norebi, they were planning what would be a devastating attack on Korachi. The Norebian warriors would arrive in the cover of night from a single direction, like a flood of water that could not be contained, drowning Korachi in its own blood. When it was over, the Korachi population would be relieved of its men, leaving the women and children to be Norebi servants of sin and farm.

Gordo, King of the Korachian Warriors, received the troubling news by messenger. Clutching the leaf of information in his massive hand, he ordered the messenger to be stoned to death while he considered his options. This would not be the first or the last battle between the Norebians and the Korachians, Gordo knew. Theirs were two farming communities in the same general society that was founded on the blood of battle, the scratching for the smallest parcel of precious, dry land. It was a society peopled with bastard sons and daughters, grandchildren of rape and horror and knives sliding across the necks of those who slept. It was all they knew.

But Gordo, who was not the smartest man but who also knew he was not the smartest man and therefore had a strange intellectual edge about him, felt this battle needed to be different. And he knew how.

He stomped from his hut, ignoring the sounds of the crazed mob and the dying messenger, and he found the weakling Haselstein near the market, by an olive tree, sucking on half of a fig. Haselstein's head was small, except for a tall, bald forehead; his knees appeared wider than his thighs. Behind him and all around the village of Korachi, craggy cliffs provided a fishbowl of protection. Norebi was a half day's walk through the hills.

"How's it coming?" Gordo asked as he approached Haselstein.

Haselstein didn't like Gordo. Or rather, he resented him. As a man without muscle or courage, Haselstein relied on the strength of thought to survive, and yet Gordo somehow used his physical strength to leverage Haselstein's strength of thought. It wasn't fair.

"How's what coming?" Haselstein asked.

Gordo boxed Haselstein's ear. Across the way, the farm girl Penelope pretended not to see. She tended to the drying fruit of her family's market stand.

"The weapon," Gordo said, "the one that will cause much destruction to our enemies."

Haselstein rubbed his throbbing ear. "Fine. It's coming along fine. We should have something in the next couple of weeks."

"That's not good enough," Gordo said, his thick beard somehow complimenting his gruff tones and bad breath. "We need something sooner. Norebi is planning an attack. We need to send a message to them, that we will not tolerate being raped and killed."

"I think that's definitely a good message to send," Haselstein almost said. Instead, he asked, "When do we need it by?"

"It must be test-fired before sundown tomorrow; they will attack at nightfall."

Haselstein shook his head. "That's impossible."

Gordo boxed his other ear. "It must be test-fired before sundown tomorrow; they will attack at nightfall," he repeated.

With both ears bursting with pain, Haselstein caught sight of Penelope's kinky black hair, her soft cheek. She had seen; so had her mother and father as they worked behind her at the stand. Several passing villagers also watched from the corners of their eyes.

"I don't mean to offend you, sir, but some things need time," Haselstein said.

Gordo nodded. He had noticed that Haselstein was watching the farm girl, that Haselstein had a pathetic crush on her, though refused to be a man about it and simply take her. He also remembered that Haselstein had promised the weapon months ago. Gordo decided that Haselstein needed extra motivation in his efforts to create the destructive tool. With Norebi planning his village's annihilation, Gordo felt his people were depending on him. He needed to ensure that his people survived.

"OK, I tell you what," Gordo said. "You get to work on the weapon and I'll bide my time with the homely farm girl over there until you're done. Maybe you'll finish sooner than you think."

As Haselstein watched in light-headed disbelief, Gordo stalked in the direction of Penelope. She saw his large, fur-covered frame approaching. Though she was diminutive, she stood tall. He grabbed her thin arm and jerked in the direction of his hut. Penelope's dark-eyed mother put delicate fingers to her concerned lips; the father frowned in the direction of Haselstein, as if Haselstein was the one taking sex from his daughter while the entire village looked in a different direction. As if Haselstein was to blame.

Haselstein called it a "catapult." Its massive skeleton sat before him on four bamboo wheels amid a collection of scraggly olive trees on the south side of the village. The arm of the weapon was erect, cocked high as if it had already tossed a two-ton stone at the approaching enemy.

He stared at the workings of the machine, a modest yet complex collection of gears, levers and a carefully placed spring, which together utilized and multiplied the power of weight and tension to create the force of at least 20 horses.

Haselstein was thinking only of Penelope. He seldom said more than three words to her each day—"Fig, please," "Thanks." But in his head, in extended stares from a distance of olive tree to fruit stand, he had shared his life with her.

"I don't think I have the energy to love you," he had said. "The love I feel for you makes me weak. I think if you allowed me to give in to it, I would fall helpless to the ground."

And she had said, in Haselstein's many daydreams, "The kind of love I feel for you gives me extra energy, so that I have the strength of many. Why don't you somehow use your brilliant mind to leverage my energy into yours? We can live and love each other forever this way."

Now, Penelope was in the brutish arms of Gordo, forced into a persuasive lesson designed to teach him—weak Haselstein—to do his work without question.

If Haselstein earlier had been telling the truth to Gordo, he might have chosen this moment to quickly and desperately work on the catapult; he might have added something here or there that would finally make it click into place, so that the slightest movement underneath would lead to another movement, and another, and another, all completed in flashes of fractions of seconds, until the catapult's launching basket was unleashed with a concentrated strength, the likes of which had never been witnessed.

But Haselstein didn't do these things because, the truth was, the weapon was already completed. Though it had never been tested, Haselstein knew by his calculations and sketches that it was capable of tossing a shoulder-high boulder a distance of 100 paces, with supreme accuracy. All that needed to be done was the actual firing. But even as Haselstein had watched Gordo drag the helpless Penelope to his hut, he had balked at performing the final ritual in the invention of a new weapon. This apathy had nothing to do with his unsaid love for Penelope.

Haselstein was burdened with a mind that witnessed the near future with precision, and he knew that once the catapult was introduced, war as humans engaged in it would change forever. The weapon was capable of killing up to 10 men with a singular, heaved stone. It could be launched every three minutes, leaving battlefields scarred with craters that would double as mass graves. It was impossibly powerful. Worse, Haselstein feared that it would soon be used so often in battle that the warriors would become comfortable with the presence of the weapon—comfortable, in effect, with the easy killings it produced. And one day, Haselstein shuddered to think, they would take the catapult away from the battlefields and aim it at a sleeping village. Its missives would cut through huts and their dreaming occupants without repentance. The survivors—men, women, and children without weapons—would run into the night, screaming, uncertain from which direction death might come.

Haselstein foolishly wondered how he got involved in such a thing—and then he remembered.

"I can invent a weapon," he had said many moons ago, "one that will destroy our enemies with ease."

He was standing at the tip of Gordo's spear as it punctured the skin on his neck. It was dark; there was a Village Cleansing under way. Haselstein, who had never fought a single battle for the Korachians, was about to die. He told Gordo of this weapon he could create, a catapult. And his life was spared.

Standing before the still weapon, his life didn't seem to matter much now. He could only think of Penelope and her pain, or worse, her newfound pleasure. Beneath the surface of his meek frame, in the back of his brilliant, pacifist mind, he felt a primal and angular need to thrust a spear into Gordo's throat.

In order to avoid being killed for lying about the readiness of the weapon, Haselstein was forced to wait until the following day, late morning, to visit Gordo's hut and tell him the news. When he arrived, a warrior-guard questioned him, told him to wait outside. After a moment, Penelope came out of the hut, clutching her furs close to her skin. Her cheeks were bruised and dusty. Her dark eyes cast over the landscape; they settled for a moment on Haselstein's. Shame connected them. She wanted to tell him that she knew it wasn't his fault. He wanted to tell her that he would take away her pain, that he would invent something that would swallow it for her. But she hurried away.

Gordo stumbled from the hut, smelling ripe and florid. His eyes held no accountability. Haselstein felt like he might faint.

"Well?" Gordo asked.

Haselstein took a breath. He was doing this for Penelope.

"I need four men to move the catapult into place. It's ready to test fire."

Gordo smiled, put a hand on Haselstein's bony shoulder.

"I must tell you," he said, "if the weapon doesn't perform well, I will kill you on the spot."

"I know," Haselstein said. "It will perform well. It is a beast of a weapon."

Gordo's eyes lit with a strange spark. The truth was, he was secretly afraid of the catapult. And his fear multiplied later that day as he stood with other warriors and a large crowd of Korachian villagers (minus Penelope and her parents), watching his men roll the catapult into a southern field.

Gordo, dressed in official warrior garb, had been in countless battles with big men, with animals, with the sharpest arrows and spears. In the darkest nights, in fields far from home, he had crushed men's skulls and tasted their inky blood. But the catapult was alarmingly huge and mysterious, like a creature formed from the land, moving slowly to the spot where it would perform its magic destruction. In that moment, Gordo admitted only to himself that if he had seen this behemoth across the battlefield from him, he might have abandoned his courageous ways and turned tail. It was something he couldn't understand.

As Gordo's lieutenants murmured their respect of the weapon, it came to rest, facing away from the village and into the field. Haselstein stood near it and told his warrior-helpers how to cock the arm with a crank and load a nearby boulder from the ammunition pile. The chosen projectile was round, smooth, very large.

Some villagers in the crowd moved closer, but Haselstein cautioned them to stay back in case it misfired. Gordo took this as a cue to speak. He raised a hand; a warrior-grunt blew an off-key horn. Everyone listened as Gordo's voice echoed off the nearby cliffs.

"The weakling Haselstein has created a superweapon that he says will ensure our survival," Gordo said. "We will see if he is telling the truth. If he is, may the Norebians feel our wrath. And if this weakling Haselstein has lied, may he feel ours."

With Haselstein trying to control the shaking of his bony knees, Gordo announced that he would remove himself from the weapon's perimeter. He would witness the firing from a point located 100 paces down and 50 paces to the left—"to better survey the damage," he lied. This was the safest point of observation, as suggested by Haselstein. As Gordo and three lieutenants made their way, the crowd grew restless.

At the target point, where the stone would land, Gordo noticed that someone had thought to create four wooden dummies holding fragile shields to the sky. They would crumble under the force of the speeding, flying, fantastically brilliant and heavy rock as it crashed to earth—what a sight to see! If it worked as planned, Gordo told his lieutenants, the weapon might even be enough to discourage the Norebians from attacking at all.

They settled 50 paces from the dummies.

By the catapult, within a ring of villagers, Haselstein raised his hand to indicate the weapon was ready to fire.

Gordo raised a spear. "Splinter the targets!" he cried.

Some witnesses reported seeing Haselstein move the catapult ever so slightly before firing. Others said it would have been impossible for such a tiny, weak man to move such a large object without help. And still others said that if Haselstein could create such a powerful weapon, one that used its own leveraging dynamics to hurl an impossibly heavy stone 100 paces, then most certainly he could also create a smaller device to move the weapon at the last moment, so that it's aim turned to a live target, spear pointed to the heavens.

What is known is that Haselstein loosed the catapult's trigger. In a windy push, the magnificent stone was soon soaring above where the crow flies, so that to the people below it became a tiny ball with which children might play, spinning, seemingly floating on the light sighs of disbelief that inadvertently escaped from the awestruck witnesses. It paused at apex, for the briefest of moments, before descending at a downward arc to a point 50 paces to the left of the wooden dummies and their now-safe shields.

Gordo and his posse had no chance. Some later remarked on the incredulity that creased his face as the stone neared, an appearance not borne of fear but of anger, that something would dare challenge him—Gordo! King of the Korachian Warriors! He died bravely, they said; and, more accurately, he died in a vapor of blood and organs, mixed with his three lieutenants, that splattered as far as the rocks on a cliff 75 paces away.

The power of the weapon had been clearly displayed—so clearly that everyone stood still for a moment, mouths open, trying to understand the sudden silence this weapon had brought to their land. And then, the death of Gordo was collectively realized. Their great leader! Murdered! In front of them! While trying to save their village through the power of technology!

There are enemies, and there are traitors, and the latter dies the cruelest deaths. For Haselstein—who swore until he could swear no more that he didn't mean it, that it was an accident, but whose claims were also interrupted once by a giddy form of laughter from him—it meant being beaten, stoned, hung by his toes and burned.

It ended for him at the center of the Korachi village. He was barely conscious; he was bloody and swollen; his teeth were chipped. But, hanging upside-down, he still had the wherewithal to pick Penelope out of the crowd, her sweet face turned sour with pain. He wanted to shout his love for her, for once, but he knew that it would only lead to her violent death. Haselstein knew better than anyone how one small action can lead to so much more.

The fire blazed beneath him, devoured him.

In all the bloody excitement, many forgot about the pending battle with the Norebians. Of those who remembered, they figured their rivals would hold off their attack for a day or two, particularly after hearing that Gordo, King of the Korachian Warriors, had been killed. Even war has certain nobility. Rescheduling the sneak attack was only fair.

But the Norebians, led by the great Warrior King Macca, decided the raid should go on. The Korachians, after all, had been planning to destroy Norebian men with a secret, horrific new weapon; why give them mercy?

It was a hellish scene that played out. The ill-prepared Korachian men (including Penelope's father) were stabbed, ripped, crushed.

And still worse, the women (including Penelope and her mother) were forced to live through it.

As the pillaging of Korachi roared into the burning night, Macca and a group of warriors made their way south. They found the weapon at the crest of a field. In the shadows created by the flickering firelight of their torches, the world's first catapult looked like a dragon, looming high, ready to strike. They approached, cautiously. One warrior threw his spear at it, and it clicked off the arm and bounced to the ground. The slumbering weapon didn't move.

Above, on a cliff overlooking the scene, Penelope felt the wind blow her dark hair. They didn't see her. If they had, she wouldn't have run. She didn't have the energy. It had been stolen from her. She felt her arms and legs go limp, and the wind picked up around her.

Jennifer Chung

Literati

Meet me between pages,
In leather-bound books
With gold embossed lettering.
In dog-eared paperbacks
With annotations running
Down slender thoroughfares
Hedged with loops and dots.

Meet me on every page
A lover whispers a promise
Or exhales in expectation or longing,
Or in satisfaction,
After a paragraph of furious back-seat sex,
Or after five pages of tantric rites,
Finally languishing in your skin.

Meet me on page 67,
The curve of my spine inside the scoop of the 6,
One leg dangling a sultry participle
Into that languid river by the savannah,
Where the porch always rots in summertime.
We'll swing by the 7, under a studded sky
And all those lovely s's.

Meet me on this page,
Having fallen into a sea of white.
Diving sidelong into the letter l
Or cannonballing recklessly into o's,
Spattering commas and quotes
Across your chest.
Kiss me quickly, before the page is turned,

With my thumb still pressed against your brow,
Your palms still lingering on my hips;

Before our tongues turn into hieroglyphs
And lips, forming plump, capital D's,
Mouth a dirge to the last vestige of speech;
Before arms diffuse into chapter headings,
Hands into a biography and Other Works;
And my name is etched in a serif font
That your eyes can no longer read.

While you were being pursued
by a phalanx of police cars
I was becoming a very popular artista

Jennifer Lawson-Zepeda

War Horses & Ashes

Twas the bleekest day—
the sun shone not with color.
My Iberian eyes looked upon chariots,
rushing into battle.

With angels' tears
fire rained upon my brethren.
And with horror I did see
desert tribes with pedigrees,
and babies ripped from mothers.

When ashen vapors cooled
and fortresses collapsed,
red seas emerged
in savage death.
A servitude of fear.

Then calls to gladiators
throughout our land,
wheels of war with fiery steeds.
War horses, well-muscled, crossed ponds
and pursued that hateful deed.

A sea of black poured to the skies,
a halo in those clouds.
With arrows poised
My brethren rode
a call to join the battle.

As angels wept again,
chariot cities emerged.
And razor sharp the blade they swung,
upon breastplates of iron
and arsenals of words.

With graves now strewn
across green and fertile land.
As poison rained, our shields held high,
the kings of kings
cried "death or jail."

I took my mount,
that Andalusian steed.
So strong and agile rode to the hills
my heart with hope.
And still no chivalry.

In noble voice
of purest form, I screamed
with flags unfurled.
Not man, nor child, nor king
heard my cries for peace, it seemed.

Jensen Whelan

Marcel's Equation

Marcel talks about big
things. He's three-quarters
stuck in supposed to be
and probably shouldn't.

According to Marcel,
the way we've been
sleeping together for
the past six months
is pretty well over the
line into definitely
not the thing to do.
That makes us either
one hundred or, if you
add us up, two hundred
percent wrong.

But we keep at it.

We met on the train,
which is not a story
that tells itself well.

"Home," I said
when Marcel asked.

"I'm going the
opposite way."

Later that afternoon,
lying in my bed,
Marcel's
hand creeping back
between my legs

like the sunlight in
through the bedroom
window, he explained
some things.

"I have a wife."

Marcel teaches math
at the public high
school, which laps
more than halfway
over into the time
we spend together.
On the days we're
apart, I imagine myself
in his classroom.
He's in front of the
whiteboard, fingernail
deep in stains from his
dry-erase pens, explaining
me to himself with
theorems, proofs, and
the occasional percentile.

Jimmy Jazz

Anarchist Think Tank

When I put out the call to assemble an anarchist think tank, the Queen of Campus Avenue showed up with exotic fish and colored rocks to line the bottom.

My lawyer brought balls with which to activate the dunking mechanism.

My daughter grabbed a brick that had been holding up her bookshelf.

Her mother suggested that we fill it with hydrogen so that the waste would be water.

The shopping cart spinster proposed that we top it with one of those pressure cooker lids that her mother used to stew marmalade, but didn't know where we could find one big enough to cover the silo.

And the bearded poet came empty-handed saying that he had set the lobsters free.

I felt awkward then, and tried to hide the turret and heavy treads behind my back.

Judd Hampton

Parts Manual

When a falling slab of steel crushes your pinky, don't scream. The guys are watching. Instead, quickly consider why you became a welder. Feel a pang of resentment towards your wife and teenaged son. Spit. Hold your hand up to see if your pinky is flat enough for the light to shine through. Resist the urge to skewer the loader operator, Garwin, (who dropped the thing) with a five-foot length of rebar. Joke about the pain (it tickles, really). Joke about your pinky now being as useless as your wife. Look beyond the shop (and that goddamn burning tire smell that won't wash off your clothes) toward the trees outside that lean so bravely into the wind.

"Sweet Holy Jesus, Russell!" Ivan Steward says when he looks at your pinky. Pay him no attention because you drive a better truck than he does.

"Ambulance's on its way, man," Cornwall, the boss, says. Laugh at his obsessive caution. You're not even bleeding. Cornwall lives in fear of the Workers Compensation Board, lawyers, phone solicitors. You fear phone solicitors too, so you don't judge him. But an ambulance seems overdramatic. You're not looking for drama. You're looking for purity. You can drive to the hospital one-handed.

When Cornwall, Taylor, and Morris try to stop you, consider running them down. You've always wanted to run them down. Now's your chance. Gun the engine. Let those big mud tires really kick up the gravel. If Cornwall, Taylor, and Morris leap out of the way, aim for that patch of aspen next to the sidewalk. Those trees are something, the way they lean so bravely into the wind. You need to take them down: Cornwall Welding Ltd. doesn't deserve the purity. You're taking the purity with you. You're on paid vacation (once you've filled out the paperwork). You've hit the jackpot, crushed-pinky-wise.

When the doctor says, "Nurse! I can save this finger!" (like one of those formulaic, white-coated, pretty-boy doctors on your wife's soap opera), resist your impulse to plunge him with the scalpel you've pinched from the drawer when no one was looking (along with the rubber gloves you'll blow into balloons later). Instead, say,

"Cut if off, please," and, "thank you." (You might as well be polite.) You won't miss your pinky. Your golf swing will feel awkward at first, but you'll get used to it. "Seriously," you'll say (because they won't believe you), "my finger feels like sawdust. Cut it off."

"Do you have a dismemberment clause in your life insurance policy?" the doctor says. Look hurt and offended and downright pissed off because you could never profit from your own misfortune. You're looking for purity in this world.

"What are they paying these days, nurse? Ten grand a finger? Perhaps, sir, you'd like me take the whole row off. Right down to the knuckles. How'd that be?" Endure his sarcastic tone, but consider his offer. You've been treading water longer than you can remember and the water's getting thick with algae. You don't have to tell him you hold three policies, or that you hold three policies because you want your family to truly benefit from the mediocrity of your death. That's just the considerate guy you are.

And when they decide they're going to save your pinky, put on a happy face because it's their job to save your pinky, and you wouldn't want them to feel substandard. Smile when they stuff your whole arm in an outlandish cast that goes all the way up to your shoulder (though they won't tell you why). You'll be off work for at least three months collecting compensation (you lucky bastard). Smile. You don't have to fake it.

When you come for your monthly checkup, and Dr. Pretty-boy (you know him as Dr. Rombs by now) is sipping a designer latté and telling you, "The bones are mending crookedly, Mr. Calberry. We're going to have to reset them," don't panic. It's a simple procedure involving a ball-peen hammer.

"Can't we just cut it off?" you say, smiling kindly as life has taught you to do.

"Don't be silly," Dr. Rombs says. Take it like a man. This is your fault after all. You will get three more months compensation and plenty of time to watch those television programs your wife always says you're missing. You can smile about that.

And three weeks later, when the intermittent stabbing pains become intolerable (it feels like a porcupine keeps tackling your upper arm), calmly notify Dr. Rombs (if he still works there). "You should have brought this to my attention sooner, Mr. Calberry," he says. There's infection, blood poisoning. Laugh and swallow another fistful of codeine. Codeine is the purity you've been looking for: you know this now.

And when Dr. Rombs shows you x-rays of your pinky, contain your excitement, because the bones are branching off, like tiny little trees leaning bravely into the wind, and for the first time since the accident, you want to keep your pinky. It has the purity your other fingers lack.

"We're going to amputate," Dr. Rombs tells you. Resist your impulse to tear out his spleen. You didn't go to medical school. Admit you wouldn't even know where to start, spleen-tearing-wise (ignore the chart illustrating vital organs: this kind of undertaking is not for you).

When you arrive at home with your pinky floating in a jar of formaldehyde that the hospital staff kindly gave you (they tied a red ribbon around the lid), show Mrs. Calberry. She'll be impressed. "Jesus, Russel! What's wrong with you, bringing that thing home?" she says. Don't turn the table over. Tell her, see, this is what you go through earning a living for your family that you love so much. And when she sighs and cracks open a new box of wine (red this time), have a drink and talk to her. She misses talking to you. And once you've exhausted all subjects (movies, needle point, her car needs an oil change), talk to your severed finger. Sometimes it just needs to hear your voice.

When you're healed and your compensation dries up and you're ready to go back to work, pay Cornwall Welding Ltd. a visit. "Economy's in a downturn, buddy. Nobody's building. Got nothing for you, man," Cornwall says. Stand over him bravely, and show him your stub. You've worked your pinky off for the bastard; he owes you. Don't show him the jar. There's been talk about you and that jar. It's not the kind of talk you want. When Cornwall shrugs his shoulders and looks at you with pity, stomp out of his office. Go ahead and slam the door. It'll make you feel better.

When you're practicing your golf swing on the ten square feet of grass you call the backyard, Mrs. Calberry starts mowing the lawn because she knows it aggravates the hell out of you. Savor your urge to club her. It's a latent response from caveman days, and you'll miss it later on, after she's left you. Mrs. Calberry mows the ten-foot square of grass with her prize lawn tractor. She keeps reversing because there's not enough room to maneuver. She also mows down your lettuce (you planted a garden after your teenaged

son said, "Dad, you're a pathetic piece of crap and I hope you die!").
You like to watch things grow.

When the bills spill over the basket on the kitchen table, don't
scream. Your family is watching. Consider those demeaning wel-
fare lines and your place in them. Feel a pang of resentment toward your demoralizing family. What will you do? You can't afford
golf. "What will you do?" Mrs. Calberry asks. Don't answer: it's a
trap. Speaking to Mrs. Calberry will make things worse. Look out
the window at the trees in the front yard that lean so bravely into
the wind. Leave the table and cuddle Pinky's jar. Tell Pinky your
troubles. Pinky's a good listener. Admit that you've been staring at
your remaining fingers in a way that makes Pinky jealous. Pinky's
given you the best years of its life, and this is how you act? Pop
some Codeine. Bury your guilt. You know what to do. It's time to
chop wood.

"Next time, and, Mr. Calberry, I certainly hope there won't be a
next time," Dr. Rombs says, "if you put the severed appendage on
ice and bring it in, nine times out of ten we can reattach it." Feel
sorry for Dr. Rombs and his workaday world, because you've found
a better way. No worker's Compensation benefits, but you'll receive
a lump payout on your three policies that you've now bumped to
five. Who needs a fourth finger, anyway? Too bad about the wedding band. You'll have to relearn your golf swing.

When your wife talks on the phone, which she does for hours
at a time, right next to you while you're trying to watch television
(because she knows it drives you nuts), fondle her breasts until she
goes away. It won't take long. You might enjoy it. Ask her at dinner,
"Why do you mow down my lettuce?" Don't wait for an answer.
"Because we eat salad every goddamn night. It drives me nuts that
you buy lettuce every time you shop. And all you do is shop." Drives
you nuts.

When the police bring your teenaged son home at three in the
morning, stoned and soaked with vomit, decide that his punishment will be to paint the house. "Make me," he says, leaning bravely over you, his blue hair flopping across his over-pierced face. Tell
the boy what he needs to hear, that you have a policy in his name.
Flash your finger-jar. Gentle persuasion is all it takes.

When you run out of money, think of plausible ways to sever
your middle finger. All you really need is a thumb and forefinger to

separate yourself from the animals. Your golf swing will suffer, but you'll adjust. Try slamming your hand in a door. Realize you didn't think that through. Dust off your circular saw: the porch needs some work.

"Really, Mr. Calberry," Dr. Rombs says. "This is becoming tiresome."

When the insurance company sends an investigator, show him your porch, the blood stains, how the two-by-four you were ripping slipped, how your saw just sailed across your finger, and how that finger rolled between the decking spacers and fell into oblivion below. "Very good, Mr. Calberry," the investigator says, penciling in his notebook. "But I'm keeping an eye on you." Salute him with your bandaged hand. Pop more codeine. After all, you deserve the purity.

When the checks arrive in your mailbox, ensure no one's watching. Yell "Jackpot!" and click your heels. Show everyone who drops by for a visit your three fingers floating in that jar. Shake the jar for them like a snow globe: you know you want to. Feel superior when they run away screaming.

When your dismemberment payments expire, don't fret. Buy more policies. Plan your big payoff: a whole leg. You can play golf one legged. That's what carts are for. It's time to sharpen your chainsaw.

When your boy does a sloppy job painting the house, make him do it again. He has to learn that there are no shortcuts in life.

Fondle Mrs. Calberry's breasts when she talks on the phone. Yell at her for buying and mowing lettuce. Pop codeine. Look at those trees out front. They're really something, aren't they? Decide that your home no longer deserves the purity of those trees. Fire up your chainsaw and lean bravely into the wind.

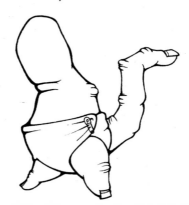

Karl Lintvedt

You Must Be Responsible For Your Mountain

It may not be the truth, but I mean it:
all things are equal with asterisks.

And as hard as your maker may try
his cultures can't train you to edit your impulses
whether it may lead you to squat in a cave
or drop a pocket sum of quarters
into the mouth of a kiosk.

A spay procedure, a neuter procedure,
a pre-interview interview
are some such examples.

You may feel it in the bloodlust that surfaces
among the company of professionals.
You may sense its spirit
foaming from a series of chrome kitchen appliances.

Pricey things that soak up the paychecks
shed by a month of honest, callused labor.
Unnatural things, the existence of which
a courtroom of gods cannot reach a verdict on.

It cannot be the truth, but I mean it:
you must be responsible for your mountain.

Kevin Fanning

Twelve Times Lost

(ii)

My father woke me up while the house was still quiet. He helped me put on my shoes and led me outside. We walked quietly along the paved road for a few minutes. The sun had begun to rise, hidden behind the clouds. We left the road when we came to the beach, and walked on the sand as the ocean fog began to dissipate. My father stopped, looking out on the water, squeezing my hand.

Just behind the edge of the fog was an old wooden galleon, wrecked in the bay. It was listing, half-sunken below the waves, torn, gray sails snapping in the wind. It looked hundreds of years old. I remember a desire stronger than any other I'd ever felt, to swim to the ship and pull myself aboard, to explore the rooms and see what had been left behind.

What is it? I asked. A ghost ship, he said, walking again and pulling my hand. I looked at him and we continued walking. I looked back at the water but the fog had moved in again, or the ship had never really existed. That's my last memory of my father. He too disappeared soon after.

"Not disappeared," my mother always says. "Left."

We live at the edge of a forest. When I was younger, it seemed as though the trees went on forever. Now I know that you can only walk for about fifteen minutes before you start seeing roofs and windows through the tree branches. It would be impossible to lose your way in there, but I was always so scared of it. You can stare at a tree all day, know every inch and indentation of its bark, but as the day ends and the light begins to fade, it will start to change shape, become something unfamiliar.

"And we're happy about it, remember?"

I don't know why he left, so I always picture my father as a skeleton in the woods. He went for a walk and got lost. He never came back. One day I will stumble over his bones, half buried in leaves.

My mother says that, if I'm really curious, I could probably find him. She has an address. She digs into a drawer and hands me a crinkled piece of paper. A P.O. Box in a city I've never heard of.

"Don't you think that's weird?" I ask. "I've never seen this city on a map. I've never heard it mentioned in stories on the news. It's two states away but I don't know anyone from there or anyone who has ever traveled there. I've never seen pictures of its buildings or landmarks."

"He gets his mail," she says, offering proof of a city's existence.

(ix)

"Let's go to the beach," came the call.

"Fuck yeah, bitch!" came the response. I believe high fives were exchanged.

The car was already driving away, backing down the driveway without us in it, the driver laughing, waving goodbye to us. We were diving into the car through the unrolled windows, scrambling into the seats.

I was sitting in the backseat. The landscape melted from houses into highways. The sun was coming at us from every direction. There were greasy shadows of finger-rubbed messages on the car windows. J and You suck. I could feel sand on the seat and floor. Someone was singing along with the radio. It felt like we were already coming home from the beach. The right feelings, the random confluence of certain moods and images, can help you create memories of the experiences you weren't fortunate enough to have.

They were yelling in the front seat.

"Well that doesn't make any sense," said the driver.

"We are doing exactly what the map has been telling us."

"Then where is the beach?"

The navigator paused, turning to look at the driver. "What are you saying, exactly?"

"I'm saying, if we're following the map, how come no beach?"

"Are you saying the map is lying? You better be saying the map is lying."

I felt really tired. You go to the beach and you run around, swim, whatever, but it's the sun that really does it to you. You want to sleep the whole way home.

"I am definitely not saying the map is lying. I am saying the navigator is a *fucko*."

The navigator sputtered in exasperation, then put his head down into the map again, more intently, as though somewhere in those blue and green lines he'd find the definition for the word "fucko."

The driver craned his neck towards the rearview mirror. "Will one of you take over navigating?" he asked.

"I do not believe this," said the navigator. I closed my eyes and rested my head against the door.

When I woke up, it was night and we were still on the highway. I opened my eyes without moving my head or body. I didn't want to move or talk or do anything that would disturb the silence in the car. I tilted my head just slightly so I could see the passing road signs. I wanted to determine if we were driving home, or still looking for the beach.

Lee Klein

One, Two, What

I'm blindsided by want. Blitzed by zeal. Speared in the back by craving. I want to throw a touchdown pass. I want to hit a tight end streaking across the end zone. I want to throw it where only the intended receiver can catch it. There are worse things, considering everything you could want. But I only want THREE THINGS. And they're not that bad. The third thing, actually, is not so good. But *the first thing*, from any perspective, is very good. The first thing being to throw a touchdown pass during a nationally televised game, preferably one of some importance. It doesn't have to be the Super Bowl. But I'd prefer to throw a touchdown pass during a must-win situation. The more toward the end of the season the better. But if I had to choose between not throwing a touchdown pass at all and throwing one, say, in the fourth quarter of a preseason game, I'd throw the touchdown pass, no matter when it was. I guess I prefer the drama. The stadium's bright glare. The roar. The falling to knees. The pointing to heaven. The post-game interview. The locker-room frenzy. The champagne shower. The jumping up and down naked. But there's not really much of that here. Not much drama, not much going on at all. Just three blank spaces I've filled with what I want.

All the lights in the bedroom are on. My husband sleeps on his back, purring more than snoring. Glossy catalogues skate the comforter across his lap, heading for the floor with each breath. I'm beside him. I grab a catalogue. I see that he's given it a good score for an electronics catalogue: 4.7. Holding it along its top and bottom ends, keeping the right margin tight, I lean over, careful not to wake him. I rip the catalogue's sharp edge across his neck, a quarter-inch from the skin of his Adam's apple. A little lower he'd have a vicious paper cut. It would seem like an accident. It would seem self-inflicted. Of course it would. But he stirs. I push the rest of the catalogues on his lap to the floor. I imagine this sounds like a squadron of geese taking off from some remote lake in his brain. He's startled awake, then settles back to sleep. I wait for his breathing to steady. I wait for the geese to land.

My husband, the man beside me now asleep, collects catalogues, or rather, he accumulates them. Towers are stacked in the corner of the bedroom, ready for evaluation. Every night it's the same: he carries a foot-tall stack of catalogues to bed, gets under the covers, flips the pages. Once he marks a cover with a score, he discards all but the best. No one ever appointed him, but he considers himself the official arbiter of catalogue quality. Perhaps this is why he never buys anything. He just flips. Buying would compromise impartiality. You have to admire that. But this bed-bound activity is not an admirable thing, this muttering to himself about favorite J. Crew seasons. I'm sure a dead man desiring a few moments of life would enjoy giving a commendable score, maybe an 8.3, to a tastefully rendered bed-linen catalogue. Only a life-loving cadaver would savor a few moments rating catalogues as though they were the routines of gymnasts, figure skaters, synchronized swimmers, whatever. But anyone who did anything of merit in their past life, anything at all, would probably commit suicide before making it through a dozen catalogues. After an hour, the lucky one reanimating my husband's body would be stuffing catalogues down its throat, the first corpse ever to choke itself to death.

I get under the covers. I cuddle up. I tuck my face deep into my sleeping husband's flannel-clad armpit. It smells faintly of fabric softener, accepts my nestling without waking the rest of him. I place a knee over his thigh to feel him closer. It's remarkable how warm he is. I realize it might seem contradictory that I get in bed and cuddle with the same man I say I want dead. I do it because I do it. Because I know him better than anyone I know. I also do it because I have a thing for his armpits.

No one else's armpits come close, not in texture, not in taste.

No one else's armpits do I want to eat out to the point of orgasm.

That's the second thing: to eat out his armpits until he comes.

Very quietly, I say into his flannel pajama top, "Honey, I want to throw a touchdown pass." If he could hear me, if he were awake, he'd yawn, look at me, slowly press an open catalogue facedown across his lap. *A touchdown pass?* he'd say, bracketing the phrase between the index and middle fingers of both hands. *Is that like "hitting a home run"? I'm too tired "to throw a touchdown pass."* Just by raising these fingers, he transforms simple phrases into euphemisms. Besides the catalogue thing, the fact that he bookends his speech with quotation-mark-making talons is another reason I'd like him dead.

It's about *complexifying*, if that's a word. Making simple things more complicated with an insanely simple action. He makes a simple phrase—"to throw a touchdown pass"—several times more complicated, simply by raising those little fingers, like they're the teeth of some venomous rodent, a hybrid of cobra and badger. What's worse is that he doesn't just let his fingers hang in the air, he accompanies them with a bobble-headed smirk. The bobbling of his head is matched in his hands, and embers of meaning are fanned as he slaps his quote-unquote talons against his palms. And this simultaneous head-bobbling/palm-slapping makes him look like an idiot imitating another idiot's idiotic attempts at snapping. It's a gesture that really pisses me off. It's especially off-pissing coming from the one man I truly need right now.

My father, the last man I truly needed, was a straight-talker. To shade his words one way or another, he only needed to adjust the force with which he rolled his words up from his gullet. Both hands always in his lap, he never arched his fingers into talons because they'd always been stuck like that with arthritis. And even if they weren't like that, he was more the type to punctuate talk with fists. If I told my father I wanted to throw a touchdown pass, the first thing he'd do, he'd be on the horn to everyone he knows, mobilizing a network of big shots, guys who pulled the strings of get-things-done masculinity, their smooth hands in ridiculously expensive deerskin gloves. Within a week, I'd be the starting quarterback for the Green Bay Packers, rolling to my right, hitting an open receiver for the score. But if my husband were to hear me when I tell his armpit what I want to do, he'd give me that two-handed, four-fingered "touchdown pass," as though it were something we could do together, to which I'd respond, "*I* want to throw a touchdown pass." I would exaggerate the "I," making it sound like the mid-air screech of a ninja taking out a no-good battalion of gangbanging toughs, who, in this case, had hidden Trojan-horse-like in the empty hull of my husband, he who *evaluates* catalogues under the covers in bed, in pajamas I mail-ordered from one of his favorites.

"I want to throw a football into the arms of a receiver open in the end zone," I say, slowly, into his armpit, letting him know I mean business.

What's that supposed to mean? he'd ask if he heard.

If he heard, he wouldn't understand. I wouldn't understand either, actually, if I were him. Some things are not so easily understood. Not even by my always-understanding husband. Not even when he accompanies his understanding with a meta-level of understanding, expressed by talons tearing the air. Actually, I know exactly what the talons mean. No matter what he intends them to say, they always seem to say the same thing. That he's *a stupid fucking white boy*. I guess I shouldn't call him that, since, to some extent, I'm the girl equivalent, but all the same. If my husband were someone who could say something real simple like *yeah*, extending this simple affirmative's syllable count from one to five, I wouldn't even care about the three things I want. If he could make *ginger ale* sound sexy, maybe I would have even fewer demands than three. But the way it is, my husband could say *suck and stroke your peach to a succulent, salacious mess* and it'd sound like *we provide dust to all those interested in comparing fiscal portfolio management and month-old danishes in an ashtray of actuarial reflux and combustible detritus, etc etc, blah blah blah, fuck*. But I assure you that things would be different if he could make *halogen lamp* sound like it involved my ass coming into contact with things that shouldn't be anywhere near it.

Even if my husband could make me come simply by saying *Styrofoam*, we'd inevitably run into problems. I realize this. We'd need other things to rely on. At least one more thing to fall back on. For each of my three demands we'd need to rely on as many *complementary stabilities*. We'd need something besides his sexy voice, something other than his armpit, which, in the absence of a sexy voice, has been the only thing keeping us together: no small feat, considering the catalogue and the talons and his monotonic way of talking. The monotone, despite being relatively benign, probably has something to do with the third thing I want.

The first being the touchdown pass.

The second being the eating out my husband's armpit to the point of orgasm.

The third being his accidental death.

It's fine by me, no matter how his death comes, as long as it happens. Preferably it'd be caused by his catalogue ranking. A severe paper cut. Anything. I realize if he were to suffer death by paper cut, however, there'd be no way I'd achieve my second goal, the eating out of his armpit to the point of orgasm (his). Just as the third goal (accidental death) precludes the second (armpit orgasm), I imagine if he were dead (by paper cut), and if I couldn't get him to come (by sucking on his armpit), then there'd be no way I'd ever throw a touchdown pass, most importantly, since it was he who put the thought in my mind long ago.

It was long ago.

When we were first married, my husband often said he would do anything for me, anything at all. Watching Sportscenter's best-of-year highlights, those spectacular plays, one after the other, quarterbacks completing long passes to sprinting receivers, bridging the distance with a spiraling ball. He said he wanted to make it so, one day, I too would drop back and hit an open receiver for the touchdown. It didn't make much sense. And it didn't have to make much sense. At the time, that's what we were about. Not quite making sense was probably a reaction to a lot of insensible things that were happening to us, to our friends, to everything. Regardless of the sense we made back then, throwing a touchdown pass seemed like something exceedingly improbable, and therefore, exactly what we wanted to do.

But that was long ago, back when we were happily applying ourselves to one another, when we'd watch football, see beauty in something I know he no longer has the capacity to see, being that he is either at work or in bed, doing the thing he does with the catalogues. And perhaps because he no longer implies that he can make the impossible probable, we've drifted apart, only interacting when I press my mouth to his armpit.

It's sad, trying to make someone remember he once believed in things that can't be done. Sometimes I hope that all this armpit sucking—the only thing I rely on right now—will make his voice sexier, and when it does, I will no longer want him dead. I'll only want two things. And what I want and what I rely on will come together to form a third stability. Something like a hovering disc of air that will take us anywhere, wherever, whenever. We'll just step on and take off.

Lisa McMann

Soap

There was so much irritation that Beulah finally called the doctor. "My eyes," she explained. "It's my eyes."

Every night during the entire month of January the frantic itching overcame her. By day there was no sign. The doctor recommended Tylenol PM. "Help you sleep, and relax you a bit," he remarked, and tossed her chart in the garbage. "Nutcase," he mumbled to the receptionist.

Beulah heard him, and she walked out without paying. The itching was inside her head now, thanks to him.

That night, Beulah lay next to her husband, exactly 18 inches from him. She could eyeball it. So to speak. And at 11 p.m. precisely, the oozing began.

For a while, she tried to ignore it. She thought about other things, like the cat, and what the neighbors were doing at that moment. She tried lying with her face buried in the pillow. When the carbon-monoxide fuzziness filled her head, she couldn't even enjoy it because of the screaming eyeballs. With fury, she rubbed them, raked them, tore at them. The oozing began in earnest, bubbling over the whites of her eyes and leaving a slimy trail down her temples, coming to rest in her ears.

Soap. It felt like soap in her eyes. The kind with granules, like at the airport restroom. Moaning brought no relief but a whap to the head from the husband.

Divert. She must divert the pain by causing pain elsewhere on her body. She grabbed the flashlight next to her bed and pounded her knee in the usual spot, bringing sweet pain to dull the creamy, stinging goo that suffocated her lids.

But she could not overcome it, and the scratching continued. She had cut her fingernails for this very reason, and she cursed herself for it. Grabbing the bear-ass back-scratcher souvenir from Six Flags, not caring that her husband actually used in on his bare ass, Beulah raked it across her cheeks, temples, and eyelids.

Blood mingled with the bubbles and, finally, she rose and stumbled to the bathroom. Gazing through scarlet foam into the mirror, lights peering through the fog, she took binoculars and smashed them into her eye sockets.

Finally... finally. From the slit next to Beulah's left eye appeared a sliver of Irish Spring, stripes still intact. With tweezers, she shakily gripped the edge and pulled. Then, pounding the other eye until a slit opened there, she did the same. Sweet Jesus! Relief fell over her like manna.

Neatly, she took the two slices of soap, rinsed them off, and set them on the ledge of the shower for morning. She wiped her face and bandaged it, and went to bed happy that her month-long-troubled eyes were healed. All the while, she dreaded the next day, and wondered... perpetual yeast infection? Boils? Hairy tongue? For the next day was the first of the month. And then she remembered the February special was the gritty crumbling teeth. Definitely not one of her favorites. Thank God it wasn't leap year.

Welcome to Crock Street

The sellers are moving because they need a larger place.

"Welcome to your new home!" shouts Jim to the buyers as they come up the walk. "Betsy's about to blow any day here!" Jim pats Betsy's enormous belly as she waves to the new owners. She is short and round, like a Weeble. She turns sideways to shake hands. Jim flicks her protruding navel through her thin smock dress and she giggles.

"You think I might have a baby plop right out my backside too?" she says with a chortle. Dan looks at Bryan, who kicks at the crack in the sidewalk.

Dan and Bryan are newlyweds and the new owners of 331 Crock Street. Their U-Haul is in the driveway. They would very much like to move in. Now. Especially Dan, since he is carrying a cage containing two rats, a ten-gallon aquarium filled with gravel, fish food, a Super Size bag of corn chips, and a Box-o-Wine. He nudges Bryan with his elbow.

"So... are the keys...?" Bryan looks around, as if the keys to the house might be lying on the lawn or perhaps hanging from the roof's gutters.

"They're on the coun—ter," sings Betsy. "Garage door opener, too. Here, I'll show you." She tips side to side as she goes up the two steps to the front door. One more step and she'd pendulum right into a cartwheel. Dan follows her, sweating now from the California sun, and Bryan holds open the door.

"I'll be in the car, waiting," hollers Jim. The others go inside.

"Whoa—ah," says Betsy, heading to the kitchen counter, where a white and red plastic bag from Target sits. "Nearly forgot myyy..."

A gush of pink-tinged amniotic fluid pours from her loins and soaks into the off-white dining room Berber, splashing the glass on the built-in china hutch. Her mucous plug bounces once on the taut carpet like a soft basketball and lands on top of Dan's loafer.

Bryan and Dan stare in shock, mouths agape, eyes like cue balls.

"Underwear," says Betsy. She snatches the bag and cradles it to her belly, blushing and twisting in her dress like a school girl who has gone and wet herself.

"Want me to... uh..." she offers, waving at the mess, then bends and grimaces with a hard contraction.

"No!" they shout in unison.

Liza Ezhevskaya

Blunt Wound Trama

—I need some ice
—Dude, man, that's gonna hurt like HELL
—Hey, could you stop talking please?
—We need some music
—Ice. Can you guys go away? I don't want anyone to watch
—Are you sterilizing the—
—Yes
—OK, good. Man, this ice is cold
—Good
—So...
—It's gonna hurt like hell
—Encouraging, really hon...
—So, are you ready?
—No
—Ready?
—No
—Yes?
—OK. Go. Do it. I'm ready.

His face gets closer as her eyes close and the music strolls into the room like a lover, the warm arms of comfort. They whisper but she doesn't understand what they say. The guitar flows like magic and her throat vibrates and she shakes and his fingers are warm on her mouth. This. Is. Going. To. Hurt. Like. Hell.

There's more of them, how many are there? I've lost count and, when I open my eyes, instead I count pores and shades of color in his eyes. Here goes. The crazy guitar riff shoots through the mellow trumpet as the metal is shoved into my skin, and there is pain and the room vibrates and there is pain and there is pain and there is—The guitar swims through my veins and dances with my endorphins, the voices mingle, there are four, I can't open my eyes, I laugh, it hurts, I laugh.

Well. It's hideous but, honey... you've got a giant safety pin through your lip.

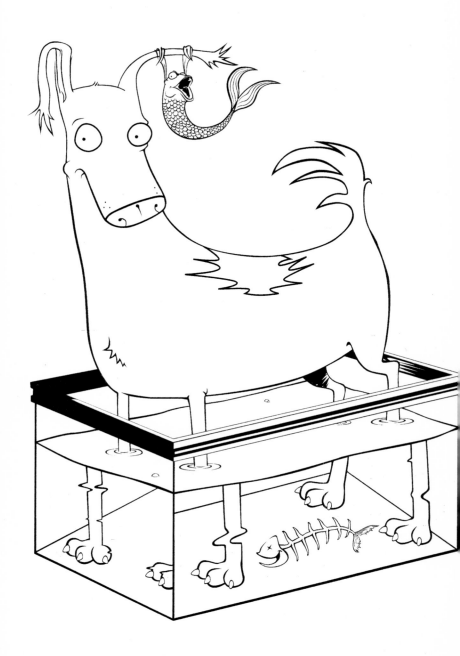

Michael Fowler

At Once Solemn, Irreverent, Moving, and Profound

I have monthly lunch dates with my friend Joe, a publisher who wants me to review his firm's books. We have a contest going. It's my turn, so I'll be taking him to the worst restaurant I can find with a literary theme that we haven't been to before. If we agree that it's no worse than the book-based place he took me to when it was his turn, I lose and will do a glowing review of his book, calling it "at once solemn, irreverent, moving, and profound." But if we agree that it's lousier than his place, then I win and get to pan his book, calling it "at once solemn, irreverent, moving, and profound." So everything rides on my choice of restaurant.

Joe has the proof of the new book under his arm, a thousand typed pages. They're dirty and wrinkled, and I can tell he's already dropped them in the street a few times. I take him to the Spouter Inn over on Main. Just opened, this is an exact recreation of the New Bedford Inn where Ishmael sups and sleeps before shipping aboard the Pequod in Moby Dick, a novel I have described elsewhere as "at once solemn, irreverent, moving, and profound." No sooner do we step in the door than whalers in period dress grab us, force grog down our throats, and rip off our clothes. "Queequeg" forces me to sing "1,000 Bottles of Beer on the Wall" all the way through while "Ahab" rapes Joe anally and then orally. I have the orange roughy.

As we come out of Spouter's, we decide to go to a quiet bar to talk out our deal. Joe's typescript under his arm now has grease, cocktail sauce, rum, and clam juice on it, and perhaps sexual fluids. At the bar, we spill pitchers of beer, drenching the manuscript and turning it into a sodden, yellow mass. We decide that the Spouter Inn was marginally more offensive than the place Joe took me last month, the Centipede Cantina, a recreation of William Burroughs' favorite eatery in Junky, that work that is at once solemn, irreverent, moving, and profound. There you gnaw on the worst cuts of poorly cooked meat with bits of feather or hoof still attached. More disgusting yet, you eat sitting at a small table looking out on an alley where rows of ragged drug addicts peer in at you through a sooty window and beseech you mutely for alms and morphine ampules. Pigeons crap on your plate through holes in the roof. And the service! I find the pork with home fries rather tasty.

Though I'll be panning Joe's book, I insist on reading it first. I'm one of those rare critics whose code of ethics dictates that, before I murder a book, I must read at least a few lines in it. So Joe hands me the manuscript, practically throwing it at me. He knows I'll still give it a chance, however. Actually he doesn't know that. Everything Joe knows about me is subject to change. We leave.

Outside, we run into an author who I reviewed some months back. He recognizes me, draws a gun, and shoots me six times. Visibly, I am devastated, a mass of blood and guts. But fortunately my essence includes existence, so I can't be killed. "Damn!" cries the hapless writer, a wreck of a man since my write-up, when he sees that my inner self is untouched by his bullets. I chuckle as he slinks off. In the literary world, I am known as The Vampire.

Back at my apartment, I take a look at the typescript that now has my blood on it and bits of my tissue along with the gin, clam juice, ketchup, pigeon shit, and everything else. And I see through the gore and the garbage that it's that one-in-a-million thing, a masterpiece. It has everything. Some values. A plot. Characters with names. Book-of-the-Monthness. Oprahbility. Page numbers. I call Joe and tell him what a find it is, and that I'm giving it my highest praise.

"You're the best," says Joe.

"There are times I am called upon to lay aside my most abhorrent traits," I answer.

I sit at my word processor. My hands would be shaking if I weren't such an old pro. I write, "I find it at once solemn, irreverent, moving, and profound."

Michael W. Graves

The Auction

Is attitude something you're born with? Or do you develop it over the years? In my case, I'd have to say it was a combination of both. Life's little tricks have certainly played their part. But I have to say that I inherited a good dose of attitude from my Grandpa.

Back in the Sixties, he was the minister for the local Southern Baptist Church in a small town down in the Ozarks of Missouri. In those days, the only pay the preacher got was whatever small change was left over in the collection plate after the church's bills were paid. Therefore, preaching was, at best, a part-time endeavor. Being a preacher, a man couldn't afford to give up his day job.

Grandpa's day job was raising beef cattle. He always made sure he kept a couple of prize-winning bulls around for stud services, and as many breeding cows as he could afford. One winter, his best bull took sick and died. So, off to the auction he went to purchase a new one.

Now the way Grandpa did things was simplicity in its purest form. He picked out the best bull of the bunch, and that was the bull he was going to have. Plain and simple. The only way he wouldn't walk out with that bull would be if someone carried the bidding so high he couldn't afford to pay for it.

As it turned out, there was another man just as determined to have that bull as my Grandpa. Since George Fleming wasn't a Southern Baptist, it didn't make no never-mind to him that Grandpa was the preacher. And about the fourth time Grandpa raised the bidding on him, Fleming sidled up to Grandpa and muttered, "Brother Jacob, I mean to have that bull and you're drivin' the price up." The expression on the man's face wasn't exactly friendly. "Now, I'd take it kindly if you'd back down and just let me have it."

Grandpa replied, "Well, sir. I need that bull just as badly as you do. And since you prob'ly got more money than I do, well then maybe you just gonna have your bull. If that ain't the case, then I guess I'm about to have *me* a new bull."

And he raised the bid again.

Fleming immediately raised the bid once again and said, "I'm warning you, Brother Jacob. I don't care if you're the town preacher or not. You raise the price on me again and you'll be sorry!" Grandpa just looked him square in the eye and raised his hand once again.

Now let me tell you a little something about Grandpa in his prime. He stood six foot, two inches tall (which for a man of that generation was pretty tall) and during the summer haying, he would pick up a bale of hay in each hand and toss both of them up onto the truck at the same time. Even in his later years, he wasn't exactly the sort of guy anyone wanted to mess with.

Fleming hauled off and hit Grandpa in the jaw as hard as he could. Grandpa's head rocked back and a tear trickled out of one of his eyes. To have that much impact on Grandpa, that guy must have hit him pretty hard. Still, Grandpa didn't go down. All he did was turn his head to the other side and tap the other cheek.

Well, all that accomplished was to infuriate the other man even more. He hit Grandpa again, only harder. And Grandpa still didn't go down. His right arm came up in an uppercut that Fleming never even saw coming. Granddad hit him so hard he toppled over two rows of chairs and sprawled out on the ground, out cold.

One of the women who happened to have been looking gasped, "Brother Jacob! I swear, you *hit* that man."

"Priscilla," he replied. "The Good Book tells us, 'If thy brother strikes thee, turn the other cheek. It doesn't say *one word* about what you gotta do if the fella is a big enough fool to hit you again."

And he raised the bid one final time.

IT WAS A GOAL OF
MINE TO BE OUT OF
CHRISTIAN EUROPE BEFORE
CHRISTMAS. I MEAN I HATE
THIS SHIT — THE LITTLE
SAD LIGHTS ON THE HOUSES

Michael Klam

The Inner *Flojo* (The *IF*)

your Inner *Flojo* lives with his sack exposed to the air
and wears a tattoo over his heart that says
Hard Work Often Pays Off Over Time
But Laziness, Laziness Pays Off Right Now

your Inner *Flojo* is a narcoleptic Buddhist
and has no qualms about rebirthing into a rhubarb,
after all, meditation is really all about sitting
and emptying your head

your Inner *Flojo* can do this

as a quantum mathematician, your *IF* states:
a penny saved is 1/258 of your next
40-ounce Olde English "800"

and as a philosopher, your Inner *Flojo* asks,
why do today what you don't give a flying fuck
about doing tomorrow?

the *IF's* motto is thus: the early bird
is the first to get shot. sleep in. and remember,
it is always better to win money than to earn it
and if anybody ever tells you differently,
they have lost touch with their *IF*.

do not listen to them. they are insane.

your Inner *Flojo* does not memorize poems
your Inner *Flojo* reads from the page
because, frankly, memorizing poems
is a pain
in your Inner *Flojo's* ass

your Inner *Flojo* loves a Big Ass
like two giant lava bubbles melding forever
in a galactic Lava Lamp, loves the song:
I Like Big Butts and I Cannot Lie
although that's the only line he has memorized
and can't really sing the song
but... he's perfectly content singing
the same lines over and over and over again

slackers unite!
(tomorrow)

in this world that demands that you be
an over-productive, underpaid and smiling wage slave,
you need
right there, standing tall in the inner sanctuary
of your dime slot or your soul
the almighty Inner *Flojo*, Regent of the Hammock
Prince of Soft Days and Shade
carrying you in his arms
to deliver you from your boss / your job

your *IF* never questions
if you do or if you don't
what if? whatever.

take a sick day
and, because lounging is love,
never, never give up
an opportunity for pleasure

Mike Coppolino

Cross-Eyed Cat

I have this cat in my house, see, and he's been peeing and vomiting all over my furniture. He's cross-eyed and slightly retarded and I've started wondering why beatniks never wrote about what happens when you invite them into your home. Sure, they write poetry and they recite it all the time, yell it in your fucking ear while you cringe and hope these unwashed scraggly beret-wearing trolls don't vomit on *you*. They tell me material possessions don't matter and they keep asking me if I want to join the communist party and become a real worker for the people, but I never see the beatnik working. He just invites people over to drink 40's and then mooches cigarettes off them. I think he's a retard but people keep telling me he's brilliant. He screams in his sleep sometimes. Lots of times, he's not sleeping, he's just walking around the room snapping his fingers saying, "It's all cool, man. It's all cool." I had to throw all my furniture over the balcony because the pee smell wouldn't come out. Now I don't have any possessions and I smell bad and they want me to join their club. They say they have a special machine that crosses eyes but I don't trust them. I think I'm an anarchist at heart, though we all seem to smell the same.

Little Man

There's a little man that lives in my sofa. He picks my pockets and eats my change when he finds some. I never catch him. It always seems like he's gone but he leaves little notes like "went to the dog races, be back at 11." Or he leaves me messages I was supposed to get three years ago, something about winning this cola contest that just expired today or something. Anything he thinks will drive me crazy. Not that I drink cola. I think he's just networking with other sofa-dwarves, taking soda cans from another one he's meeting when he makes those dog-racing excuses. I know he can't bet. I even suspect he's much smaller than an actual dwarf. Almost as small as a fictional character yet big enough to eat a quarter. Now they have those new metal dollars out and I'm getting really afraid I might go broke. I think I'll have the tailor put zippers on all my pockets. But if I do that, he'll just start using the phone or watching the home shopping channel. I have some credit cards missing already but they always come back. I think he's stealing the numbers to fuck with my credit rating and now I live in fear. How else should I explain those collection notices and that package of commemorative Wizard of Oz dishes I got from the Franklin Mint?

Paul A. Toth

Satellite Girl

Everything came down on Wayne that morning, everything and everyone. First his mother called with the watch-what-you-do, the don't-do-this-but-please-do-that, the what's-wrong-with-Texas and the why-California? On and on. Then the magazine guy came, some dumb college kid practically rifling through his house for nickels and dimes when Wayne had ten times said there was no money for magazine-subscription fundraisers, not for spring break trips, not for trips to the moon. Then his sister called and yammered on about how she had a plan, that she was selling the trailer, moving to Georgia, buying a house, finding the best school in the state, concentrating on her kids because the kids are the future and her life was over, and that he'd better stay away from white girls like Cheryl because white girls had gotten him into the mess he was in now. Then Cheryl called. She wanted to go to Venice Beach because her kid had lived in California five years and still hadn't seen the ocean. She let him know there was no bus to the beach from the Valley, that somebody like Wayne couldn't be expected to spend a day with his girlfriend and her kid when all he cared about was s-e-x, and that he'd better keep his voice down because her daughter had good ears, satellite dishes. And when he advised Cheryl that his '94 Nova really didn't care for trips to the Valley and the ocean and back to the Valley and then back to Los Angeles, nearly a hundred miles in one day, she let him know that was why he still drove a '94 Nova: no ambition. She hung up, no doubt waiting for him to arrive like the bus that didn't go from the Valley to Venice Beach.

He drank three beers in ten minutes. Calming down, he thought to himself that Cheryl was a good bet, better than the last three, but there was the kid, that damn kid. How in the hell would he entertain her all day long? He couldn't come down to her level, nor talk to her like some dad. All he could do was wait for her to fall asleep, then bury his head in Cheryl's arms and hope the next day never came. When morning arrived, he'd race out of that apartment faster than any kid weighed down by satellite-dish ears could run.

He found the keys to the Nova underneath the highlighter-stained classifieds. "A man with no ambition wouldn't highlight the want ads. Probably wouldn't even glance at 'em," he thought.

As usual, the Nova required turning on the heat so the temperature gauge dropped below the car's fever range. He passed hundreds of shops beyond his means. He imagined their owners sprinting from the stores and yelling, "Bus driver! Nova owner!"

The drivers who edged within half an inch of his bumper seemed to believe their cars could pass through his like they were in the Twilight Zone, BMW=MC². He tossed a cigarette butt and hoped it would smoke the Valley.

At every stop, the car's temperature rose, reminding him of his reward for the ambition-free life. He imagined Cheryl's feet swinging with impatience, her toe-nails painted green for "Go, go, go." But the harder he pressed the accelerator, the higher the gauge slid into red. Had he taken the freeway, the engine would have suffered a heat stroke.

And then, at a corner, the car died, right under a green light, as if Cheryl's impatient foot had come down and stomped him at the juncture of Where-the-Hell-Are-You Avenue and Don't-Bother-Calling Boulevard. He left the car parked there. He had heard the noise the engine made three times before, two Vegas and a Chevette. The Nova would be towed away, never to be claimed. Some citation or another he couldn't afford would be added to his record. But if the cops came, he was going to jail for one of his other twelve violations.

A mile away, he found a pay phone and called Cheryl.

"I knew this would happen," she said. "Meet me at the mall, in the center by the big fountain."

"But how—"

"I don't care how."

He waited for an hour before the cab picked him up and took him to the mall. He blew the first fifty bucks of his unemployment check on the fare, thanks to the traffic jam his Nova had created.

As he walked to the entrance, he tried again to figure out what it was about malls he hated. The sad music the stores played, as if trying to depress him? The merchandise he couldn't afford? The sparkle and shine? That everyone seemed to have satellites for ears and could feel the vibration of his discomfort?

Cheryl and the girl were waiting at a specially-constructed pool with a hundred other mothers and babysitters and kids. He shook his head, thinking, "Lord only knows what my punishment will be." Then he saw that the kids held fishing rods. He saw big and little fish in the water, swimming for their lives from a tide of hooks and bobbers.

Cheryl's arm was in his hand. He was careful not to squeeze too hard. He knew she expected the worst from him, that any day now he might blow under the weight of his ambition-deprived world.

"What the hell is this?" he said.

"We can't take Cammie to the ocean, so we're taking her fishing. Or is that too much to ask?"

The girl watched her bobber skitter along the surface, bumping into the other bobbers that polka-dotted the water.

"It's not so bad," he told himself. "It's not as bad as you think."

He looked at his watch. It would be at least six hours before the girl—Cammie, he reminded himself—fell asleep.

"So how are you getting home tonight?" Cheryl said.

"I'm not."

"Oh, yeah? And tomorrow?"

He shrugged. He watched Cammie struggle to free her line from some other kid's. He was thinking, "I can't enter that scene. I'll stay right here. She'll give up."

Cheryl said, "Can't you get off your ass and go help her, for Christ's sake?"

Before he could absorb having entered the mob of children, he was unraveling the lines.

"You drank beer," Cammie said.

"Yeah, I drank a beer."

"More than one."

"Okay, I drank more than one."

"Why?"

"I'm not having a very good day," he said, tossing the freed bobber back into the water.

"But why?"

Before he could try to summarize the god-awful day, Cammie was watching the bobber again.

"We'll give her a while," Cheryl said, "then maybe get some food. You got any money?"

He was going to explain how, after the cab ride, he really couldn't afford to feed all three of them. Cheryl bit her fingernails, as she always did when demanding the answer he was not planning to give.

"Yeah," he said. "We'll get something to eat."

Suddenly, there was a splash in the pool. The mothers and baby-sitters and children cheered. Wayne expected some fish mascot to come out of the water, but instead he saw Cammie trying to hoist a fish into the air, her line about to give.

"Damn," he said, the fish on the line ten times the size of any he had ever caught. His was a life of blue gills, not trout or whatever the hell it was.

"Go help her," Cheryl said.

When he arrived beside Cammie, an assistant was already freeing the fish from the hook. After the fish slid out of Wayne's hands, the attendant handed a stuffed animal to Cammie and said, "Congratulations, little girl" for what must have been the ten-thousandth time that day.

"Look," Cammie said.

Wayne wanted to say "wow" in a way that sounded like the word's meaning but he couldn't. He hadn't felt that way in so long, "wow" might as well have been French.

"Let's celebrate," he said.

Cheryl didn't look exactly proud of him but she wasn't frowning either. They went to the food court and sat at the counter. Cheryl and Cammie ordered hamburgers and soda. He was glad to see the place had a permit to sell beer. Malls had come a long way since his last visit. He ordered a Miller and ate some of Cheryl's fries.

"So how come we didn't go the ocean?" Cammie asked.

"You caught a fish," he said, surprised he had spoken first rather than waiting for Cheryl as he normally did. "Isn't that good enough?"

"Yeah, but I wanted to see the ocean."

He thought for a moment. "You see that fountain there?"

She nodded.

"Well, where do you think those fish come from?"

"I don't know."

"They come from the ocean."

"Wayne," Cheryl said, tapping her ears as if to signal that Cammie could hear so far inside him that she'd know he was lying.

"Yeah," he said, "there's a river that goes from that fountain, down under the mall, and all the way to the ocean. That's an ocean fish you caught, girl."

"Really?"

"Really."

"Hmm," Cheryl said.

He looked away at the after-work shoppers. The music no longer bothered him. He had already spent money he couldn't afford to spend. The sparkle and shine made "wow" an English word again. He felt no discomfort for anyone with satellite ears to detect.

Cheryl was biting her fingernails.

"What's for breakfast?" she asked.

Ryan Kennebeck

A Girl and Boy, Late Teens, Eating Sandwiches

"My favorite dream... ever?" the boy asks, and the girl nods as if to say *yeah, that's the one*. "Okay. Okay. I was... fifteen, I think. And I was in school—but it was like... the last hours before winter break, and no one cared, right? I skipped my period after lunch and went into the library, where there were these... like... amazingly comfortable couches, right?" And the girl nods as if to say *sure, couches*. "So, I laid down on one of these couches, not really planning to go to sleep or anything but... it must have been the smell of the library or the books or staring up at the ceiling—which all have the same effect on me as a lullaby—and I do kinda fall asleep. But it's... one of those quick naps that seem to... swell out of clock time, into something else, right?" The girl nods as if to say *sure, something else*. "I don't know how that works. When you dream during short naps and they seem to turn time to taffy... like Narnian time. Ever read The Chronicles of Narnia?" *Sure, Narnia*. "Okay, so, I fell into that... like... eternity of stolen sleep and I start to dream... well... okay, I start to dream that I'm being spun around by my feet. Really fast. I mean really fast." *Sure, really fast*. "And everything is a blur of colors, flashing light, dark. So, for what feels like hours, I'm just contented in being spun. Really fast. And I get that feeling where all the blood rushes up into my head and my ears are pounding, but I'm not getting sick. Like, not throw-uppy sick, right?" *Sure, not throw-uppy sick*. "But I finally kinda do that thing where you lift your head and look up, you know, straining your neck, fighting the G's, and I don't see anything except for this... shock of light. But I know what it is. It kicks me in... like... between the eyes. Like emotion. And it's clear that God... yeah, some kind of God is spinning me around by my feet."

The girl doesn't nod. She smiles vaguely, slowly.

The boy continues; "But just as soon as I realize this, I... I wake up, right? Just, bam—God's spinning me around by my feet and my eyes pop open. I'm just popped back into life, like... burnt toast or... or something. And I'm staring at the ceiling—and... get this... the ceiling is spinning. Like the world does when you're done spinning.

Like... when it's catching up with you. It's spinning like a record, like a top, like a possessed head, like a... like a... I get dizzy, okay? And then I roll off the real comfy couch, and onto the ground with a... like a waahh! or some kind of yelp."

The girl looks at the boy, scrunches up her nose, "Really?"

"Really."

"Okay," she says. "Now, so... juxtapose that with your favorite memory."

"Uh..."

"It's a game." She says. "You tell me your favorite dream, and then your favorite memory, and then we see how they connect. You know, since, in some ways, they're kind of the same thing. Placing them over top of each other is just like... well like seeing your past or... yourself through 3-D glasses."

"Okay." The boy thinks, kind of smiles. "Um..."

"Don't think about it too hard." She says.

"I'm trying not too."

"Okay."

"Uh..."

She frowns; "Say something!" then kicks his shin.

"Oh…" Wince. "Okay, I got it. I got it. It was... it was... oh, probably when I was eight or so. Or seven. Or six. And it was at one of my mom's softball games, which would be, like, on Thursday nights, after school. And Dad would come get me from school and bring me over to this park where they'd always play. And we'd have a picnic…" *Sure, Picnic.* "…PB and J's. Classic, maybe a little milk, maybe a few ants. And we'd always have it on this ratted up old blanket that—no—it couldn't have been that ratted up. It was, kind of beige, stained by spilt milk, it was kind of musty. But, there was no better place to watch the clouds pass. You know, feeling the grass crush down beneath you... rustling like a... language. Okay. Okay. But after eating, and after I had run myself out and I'm just lying around on the lawn, sweating, itching from exertion and being cut up by the grass, Dad would... how do I explain this. I'd sit down in the middle of the blanket, kind of *zazen* style, and then Dad would take the corners of the blanket and pull them up together, so... like a rucksack." *Sure, rucksack.* "And then he would take those ends and... and he would swing me around." The boy pauses, gets lost. "Christ."

The girl makes an 'ah' face, with slightly opened eyes, slightly parted lips. Looks like she's pulling back from a kiss.

"But... I can still remember how that felt." The boy says. "Being swung around inside that blanket. Like, in this perfectly enclosed egg, flashing greens and sun and yellow and trees. And being totally helpless and not minding... like childhood."

"Oh," the girl says. The boy looks at her and he realizes that he hasn't really been looking at her. "Oh, baby," she says, "you're not that hard to figure out."

Of Time

Freshman year English class
I carved this poem
into my desk

Poetry is to words
what spitting contests
are to spit.

I carved the words deep
with the sharp end
of a broken comb
which I kinda snapped in two
because along the top
was written a one-word poem

Unbreakable.

Maybe my poem
is still there.

Someone sitting in class
reading it with stoned eyes
or tarred fingers
right now...

or right now...
or right now.

Maybe they're laughing
or blinking
or yawning
or asleep
head curled on arms
and drooling.

(Bastards.)

I didn't like the class
or the teacher (bitch)
she annoyed me.

All her prompts were geared towards
eliciting sap about
dead grandfathers or
barely attempted suicides
(quarter bottle of aspirin—
—kitchen knife wrist slice)
under-over-unlearned-from-love.

There was a girl
in front of me.

I didn't really know her
but she was always bundled up
against the cold
even in the sweaty summer
and she wrote on her shoes
with a marker that had
a sailor's mouth.

(She smelled like raked leaves,
I don't know how.)

And when we were supposed to write
a love story for class
she wrote a horror story
where this guy was fed his own heart
with chives by a madman in a chef's hat
and people winced when she read it
aloud.

Sometimes
when I tell this story
I say that I laughed
but really
I winced too.

And with that wince
I think I fell in love
with her.

Well...

Only the sort of love
that makes me think about her
every once in a while
at random
and this is the sort of love
that never leaves.

The sort of love
that sneaks
her in.

I think I want her
at my funeral
maybe in the back somewhere.

At the end of the school year
during a movie we were watching
while our teacher (cunt)
smoked gossip outside
the girl turned around
and read the poem I was scratching into my desk
with the sharp end of my broken comb.

I looked at her
stopped scratching words
and eye contact
like pause button.

She smiled
said:
"that's
forever
y'know?"

Savannah Schroll

Famous

It was 6:30 when he woke. He lifted his satin eye mask and looked around the room. For once, he was alone. Disappointed, he sat for awhile in the sheets, playing with the satiny folds, watching how the half-light coming in between the velvet curtains played against them. He suddenly touched his nose, feeling around the tip, the sides. He did not lay a hand on his cheeks. But he felt something there. A bump perhaps.

He threw back the covers and strode across the room, his robe and its belt fluttering behind him. Seated in front of a large round mirror, he clicked a tiny switch at its base and sixteen pink-tinted bulbs instantly illuminated its circumference. Reflected there was the face he had gone to bed with. Nothing had softened or shifted. No marks or blemishes were apparent. It was unstable perfection.

On the vanity top was a pair of cotton gloves. He put these on and began to touch his nose again, pushing lightly on the tip. To the left. To the right. He remembered having dreamed that it had changed in the night. The maids had come in to make his bed and found him asleep in his red, sequined military jacket with nothing but a vacant cavity where his nose had been. It had melted inward like a spent candle in birthday-cake icing.

He sat for half an hour in front of the vanity mirror, peering over an entire landscape of cosmetic jars, and ritually examined this face, not yet entirely familiar to him since the last surgery. He tried to memorize the details, so he might know if something had changed. His fingers stopped at his chin and languorously traced its contour. He'd done well to add the cleft. It was a chin that was classic, a chin that lured, a chin that might arrest the malignant intentions of influential men with its silent resolve. A hero's chin. Yes, looks were everything, the only thing that insured your continued survival, determined your experience of external reality, drew people to you, gave you complexity, made people want to know your story. Suddenly disappointed with what gazed back at him, the too-vivid figure that blinked when he blinked, he pulled a black scarf over the mirror and clicked off the pinkish-yellow illumination.

The wonderful thing about children, he thought, his mind quickening, was that most of them accepted all things. So, no matter that his angles were all wrong, that he might spontaneously develop some horrible rash. If they were young enough—they must be young to be courtiers in his entourage—they would not reject him. He did try to be perfect for them, though. And before he went to see them, he prepared as carefully as one might for a lover. Even now, he applied kohl to his lower lids, staring wide-eyed through the dark, gauzy material covering the mirror. He swabbed his cheeks with isopropyl alcohol, put on a pair of rubber gloves from the bottom bureau drawer and applied some cream from a small purple tube. Over this, he brushed berry-colored blush. He gave himself three quick sprays of White Diamonds from a turquoise atomizer, one squirt for each side of his neck and another on his breast bone, where his skinniness made it overly prominent. He looped a careless knot in the belt of his dressing gown and took one last, narrow-eyed side glance at his hazy reflection in the vanity mirror. His lip curled, his brow furrowed, he tugged at the belt and let out a stage-practiced howl. He was ready now. Ready for them.

A veritable facsimile of Versailles, his home contained as many decorative curiosities. Rococo sculptures of naked men, satyrs, and nymphs lined the walls like debauched sentries. A long row of chandeliers glittered overhead. Their prisms, dangling like heavy dew, like viscous raindrops, tinkled slightly, audibly, and threw colored geometric shapes onto the walls. He walked beneath them, looking up rapturously, mouth open, arms outstretched. He cupped his pasty white hands with their strange, naturally purplish nails and pretended to catch them. Those standing within ear shot might even have heard that he was laughing a little. Giggling.

The maids snuck into parallel hallways in order to avoid passing him, but he did not seem to notice. He was looking for the children now. He quickened his pace, adding a skip.

Wouldn't they be happy to see him? Wouldn't they.

Scott Halligan

The Travelers

Into the strenuous briefness:
    Life.

I reeled at incredible speed—in this part of the stream the
    traffic left shooting stars forgotten in its wake.

The travelers swarmed thickly,
    pressed forward with startling urgency.

The navigation was a nightmare:
    Dodging first rainclouds, spelling books,
    maneuvering deadlines, bills, dodging meteors,
    car parts, aluminum cans.

The field here was littered with space junk,
    and Tragedy.

There a rare traveler sped by, cruising at optimum velocity,
    successfully navigating the field at the highest speed
    possible. A marvel. I applauded him.

But most travelers flew unreasonable flight paths,
    at unreasonable speeds.

There, one just spun out. There, a bloody collision. There, a
    nosedive, there, an engine stall. And there one backward
    traveler, heading for his doom—Crash!

Some travelers dodged imaginary obstacles and didn't seem to
    notice when the meteors struck them,
    removed large portions of their bodies.

Some flew backwards.

Some travelers flew erratic paths, speeding forwards,
    backwards, high and low, pushing the envelope.
    These the police shot down.

At the bottom, crawl the crash survivors:
    Sometimes one can get up and run and learn to fly again.
    (but not often)

Sometimes they claw at low-flying travelers.
    Sometimes they sit and wait for all the travelers to pass.
    And for the great grandfather clock to come and gather
    them up in his hands.

(and many of the travelers
    flew backwards)

There, a peculiar traveler flying on his back in black robes,
    hands praying, eyes closed. And bumped on the head.

The destiny-bound traveler of optimum velocity had a different
    kind of faith, I thought.

Observing the lamentable travelers,
    I reeled at incredible speed.

"Those poor, stupid sons-of-bitches," I thought, and—Whack!
    A meteor struck me square in the backside.

Stephen Ausherman

Unqualified Angel

My guardian angel, before he died, was a lithium addict, and worse, a poet. His job now, of course, is watching over me, which shouldn't be so difficult. I don't play any dangerous sports or even move around all that much. But that's still no excuse for his habitual tardiness. He just shows up when he feels like it—no clock to punch—and he stands around wringing his hands and slapping at invisible insects on his neck.

He'll burn through a year's worth of sick leave by mid-February, then, every other week or so, he'll take a personal day. He usually spends them down at the docks; he won't say what he does there. He sleeps on the job, too. And when he sleeps, he mutters on about Christmas and betrayal. Those are the only words I can pick out of his sentences, for when he sleeps he clenches his jaws and affects a thick Irish brogue I never hear when he's awake.

Once I asked him why he bothers to show up at all. He said it's his job and he can't get out of it, but he doesn't know how he got stuck with it. "At first, I thought it was Hell," he told me. "But they explained in the orientation that Hell doesn't really exist. It was just an idea the Messengers cooked up because they felt mankind lacked a sense of irony."

He's not in purgatory either. "Jesus frowns on that word," he said when I suggested it over breakfast. "And, God as my witness, you do *not* want to see Jesus frown." We split the last crueler and never brought up that subject again.

I can't keep any wine in the house because he'll drink it all, and he's a horrible drunk, all maudlin and angry and full of self-pity. I've suffered through his monologues seventeen times already, his bitching and moaning about how he was born a saint, but the world spilled poison on his soul.

"Transpose a single letter," he's fond of repeating, "and a saint becomes a stain."

He'll go on and on about how he fought the corruption braided into his DNA. He tried vows of chastity and silence, then blamed his failure on sexual addictions and a pathological compulsion to

111

read bad poetry in public.

It did not make him a better person.

"I've suffered a miserable life," he'll tell me again and again. "But not a moment of it was as wretched as my station in death."

Watching over me, he says, is a damningly dull job, duller than any job I've known. I sometimes feel sorry for him. The only thing duller than a dull life is watching someone else's dull life. But then he'll start harassing me to pick up the pace. "Take up bullfighting," he says. "Practice a religion that involves snake handling. Consider a career in demolition."

My guardian angel never worked a day in his whole sorry life and he thinks he deserves a better job now that he's dead. He's not qualified for the one he's got. Sometimes I think I should become a poet and demote him to my muse.

Nobody Appreciates My Talent

I

Dear Steven,

Per your letter dated March 8th, I have decided to decline your request to lend my name and a subsequent small quote to be included as a blurb on the back of your latest book. While we have been friends since college and I have enjoyed some of your writing (particularly the pieces which don't take long to read), I must refrain from forwarding on a passage of praise, as I feel I may lose my wife if I were to act otherwise. As you may or may not recall (we're still uncertain as to your level of inebriation), your behavior at my recent wedding was, well, all that can be said is, "appalling." Your singing along with the organ at the beginning of the ceremony (complete with vulgar "new" lyrics to the classics we'd chosen), the heckling (particularly your insinuation that "the both of us better get a move on 'cause we're just getting uglier by the minute"), and the inexcusable, nauseating laughter you emitted when seeing our ring-bearer, my wife's impishly small nephew, whom, I'll have you know, has a severe glandular problem. All of these, among other incidences, were simply uncalled for. I won't even begin to describe the feelings of utter humiliation we and our guests suffered at the reception, nor will I even touch on your unannounced arrival and subsequent weeklong stay at our honeymoon suite in Barbados. I'm sorry, Steven, but my wife, whom I cherish with utmost devotion, has never let me forget these events and has, on more than one occasion, encouraged me to sever ties with you completely. While we certainly have our history, I'm afraid that I must agree with her, simply with the understanding that her finding of a single e-mail from you or, God forbid, a voice mail, would lead to unnecessary marital hardships and possibly towards divorce proceedings. That said, please take care. Just take care somewhere else, okay?

Sincerely,
John

II

Steve,

When I received my mail this afternoon, not in my most wild of day dreams could I have suspected to find a letter from you. Yet there it was: my name in the addressee section, and the name of my former student, and no less, of the one I still refer to in my classes as "The Student Most Oblivious To The Structure of the Written Word". Why, before receiving this letter, I'd almost come to forget that you were actually a living, breathing entity, as the aforementioned title I'd been using, along with your former papers I'd been handing out to my incoming freshmen, had served for so many years as a kind of fictitious warning à la the boogeyman of prose ("Watch out," say, "or you could one day be churning out vile substance like this!"). I found it almost laughably impossible to see your name there in front of me. But with that unmistakable, nearly unintelligible handwriting, I knew the correspondence truly must be from you, the only student I've had who'd run out of my classroom, sobbing uncontrollably after having wet himself for no apparent reason. Upon reading your letter, often puzzled by the many misspellings, dozens of sentences seemingly without any correlation to those surrounding them, and your (very familiar) lack of punctuation, I deciphered that you were requesting that I write a blurb in praise of your new novel (which was said to be included, though was not). I took some moments of consideration, but then realized that this must be some sort of prank. Or, and I fear this might be a very real truth, it represents a very cryptic piece of correspondence which serves as evidence of your slipping grasp on sanity, thinking yourself a talented author. Whatever the reasoning behind the fictionalized request, I feel it necessary to respond to you, presumably now in captivity at one of the many state-funded mental institutions, and inform you that I appreciated hearing your name once more and, if this will do you any good, got a hearty laugh out of your letter.

All My Best,
Jonathan

III.

Steven,

As the Greek's said so eloquently back in their classical era of un-abashed knowledge: "No."

Sincerely,
Martha

IV.

Mr. Delahoyde,

In response to your letter RE: Writing A Blurb For My Latest Book, dated March 19th, 2002, we at McHannon, Jacoby, and Miller, who serve as legal council for your ex-wife, Ms. Diana Rothstein, would like to remind you that the court-ordered restraining order (#142J2011aa), obtained by our firm upon Ms. Rothstein's request, clearly states that it applies to written correspondence, along with all other methods of communication. At this time, Ms. Rothstein does not wish to seek litigation against you but wishes to remind you only that any further instances will result in swift legal action by our firm.

Sincerely,
David Jacoby
Partner
McHannon, Jacoby, and Miller

V.

Steven,

In reading your letter, and then the copy of your newest novel, I was reminded of a quote I'd heard once, maybe by Mark Twain, I don't remember really. But it basically went something along the lines of, "You plagiarizing bastard!" I think no time more than the present does it apply more aptly. This book that you've sent reads almost identically to an earlier work of mine, appearing so similarly that I believe all you have done is switched the letters around in some of the character's names. What's more embarrassing is even then, you do it somewhat sporadically, as in your character Mrs. Srace Gmith, who halfway through the book, returns to being named "Mrs. Grace Smith," my novel's heroine. And perhaps even worse than this is the very title of the book, entitled *Fourteen Trips To Kingston*. Mine, you'll no doubt remember, was *Thirteen Trips To Kingston*, titled as such because each trip corresponded to a chapter. Your title leaves one extra, chapterless-trip. Mr. Delahoyde, I am an old man and I realize that I don't have much time left on this Earth, so instead of calling my lawyer or my publisher, or someone else who would probably make both our lives a living hell, I will leave you with a bit of sound advice concerning this business of writing, particularly in regard to plagiarism. 1) Be consistent with your alterations. 2) If you are too lazy for that, at least change the title. 3) (and this is perhaps the most important point): Don't send the damn thing to the person you stole it from, asking them to sing your praises. In short, use some common sense.

Best of luck to you,
Timothy

Things to Say about Books I Haven't Read

The first point is the boyfriend thingy but I'll skip that for now.

The second point is that I'm at the bank and the girl in front of me is reading the same book that Janelle is reading.

This reminds me I'm running errands, which makes me think of cranberry juice extract, which reminds me of Janelle, her urinary tract infection, her 'ex,' and the fact that I am running errands.

The third point is she looks real young. She's probably twenty/twenty-one, I'm guessing in college. She holds the thick paperback by her side, one finger marking a page.

When she looks back at me, I say, "You know—everyone I know is reading that book."

"Really?" she asks.

"Yeah. Why is that?"

"Hm," she says, "I don't know."

I shrug, "It's long."

"Yeah," she looks at the cover of it, "but it's good."

"Oh, I know."

"You've read it?" she asks.

Now, see, I've almost got her. "A while ago," I say.

The teller says, "Next," and we both look up.

"Go ahead," I nod.

"Thanks," she smiles. At the window she smiles again, over her shoulder.

The fourth point is she follows me out of the bank.

I hear feet shuffling across the wet cement behind me and turn around. "Hey."

"Hey."

"What else you read by him?" I ask.

"Oh, like three others. I can't remember all their titles."

"Yeah, he's good."

We both stop walking. She flicks her hair out of her eyes and looks at her feet. Standing on her heels, touching her toes together she says, "It was on Oprah."

"What?"

"The book. It was on Oprah."

"Oh. Yeah. That's it. Book of the month and all."

"Yeah, I know. Embarrassing."

"I kept wondering why everyone was reading it."

For a second, the girl doesn't say anything. She just stares down, shrugging her shoulders, snapping gum.

I can't think of anything else, so I say, "John."

"Oh, yeah," I think she is going to shake my hand but she says, "Steph," smiles, "—anie. Stephanie."

"You read a lot Stephanie?" I ask.

"Some. I'm very analytical," she pauses here, makes sure I'm listening, "my boyfriend is the creative type."

I ignore her. I live by a strict don't ask/don't tell policy but, then again, I wasn't the one following her across the parking lot.

I look over at the silver Benz and push a button on the key. The brake lights flash once.

She looks at the car and then down again at her feet. "That's you?"

"Yeah. Ever driven one before?"

"No."

The fifth point is that my father is out of town. He has shelf after shelf of books; novels, poems, short story collections, criticisms, philosophical texts, theological texts, how-to and self help texts—everything.

At first, she sits, her knees angled in, almost touching, but then gets up and walks over to the shelf. She pulls *Travels With Charlie* and looks at the back of it. "Good?" she asks.

"Yeah," I say and hand her three fingers worth of Seagrams 7 in a coffee cup.

I sit down then on the couch and lean back. She follows me, book in one hand sipping from the cup and kicks her shoes off.

"Read some of it to me?" I ask.

"Really?" She draws her chin back close to her neck but says, "Okay," and I laugh.

I move close to her, read over her shoulder and after a few lines I can see goose bumps rise a little on her neck. By the middle of the second paragraph we have kissed briefly, our lips touching quickly and parting. She starts kissing me a little more and a little more and by the end of the page her tongue flashes into my mouth. I take the book from her lap, close it, and rub her there.

Her cell phone starts to buzz, vibrating through her purse on the glass coffee table, but she doesn't seem to care. She just keeps kissing me.

The last point is that her cheek is on her palm and her elbow is on the pillow and with her free hand she runs her nails down my chest.

Her eyes are stoplight green. They are hard to look at, glittering, flashing, pretty even with her eyeliner dotted from sweat. I look at her chin instead, rubbed raw in spots from my scruff.

"What time do you have work?" I ask.

"Not until seven," her hand slips down below my belly button. I tense up and she laughs, scratches my chest again.

I like her nails on my chest, I even kind of like her being there, but now, now my phone is vibrating and I know it's Janelle, I know it's past four, and I know she needs her car back.

I think again about the cranberry juice extract and look up at the girl with my mouth closed and raise my eyebrows.

I don't have anything else to say about books I haven't read.

Dreams about Steven Who I Hear Looks Just Like Me

I keep having these dreams about Steven, who I hear looks just like me, where I'm fucking Janelle and he's on the other side of the door, banging on it, telling her, "Janelle, I got to get in, I need to see you," and she keeps twisting up (she's on her belly) and putting her hand on my chest, yelling, "Hold on!" and, "Just a minute, sweetie," like he's got all day, sitting out there, and the dogs—his dogs, really—are barking and they keep jumping up on the bed—his bed, really—and they run from one side of us to the other and jump off the bed and I'm kind of caught in this position where I want to get off her, so I hit it a little bit harder, a little bit faster, and try to concentrate a little bit more on the idea that this whole thing ought to be real exciting but all I'm really doing is thinking about how there are three ways out of the room: the one into the backyard, which would present problems of getting out of the backyard, or the one that leads into the garage, which presents problems because that's where all Steven's stuff is being stored and I would probably knock over a lamp or trip over a box or his motorcycle or his skateboard (his snowboard's in my trunk)—or I could just walk out the front door, which is the one he's banging on or leaning against I'm guessing because he's all quiet and then he bangs on the door again and I'm thinking he must be coming down or just down or about a day down because in the other dreams he's tweaking, eyes all big and black like a motherfucker, and he's got this really, really long .357 and I'm fucking Janelle—only we're not at her(/his) house, we're over there at the Chateau Marmont and for some strange reason my one friend Red, the one that looks like a sunburned Stanley Tucci, is sitting in front of the TV with Steven's Play Station 3 drinking Heineken and Steven doesn't knock, he just comes right in and I roll off Janelle and he puts the barrel of his gun real hard up against my temple and he tells Janelle, "Get back to the fucking house, J," just like that, and then he looks at me with the fucking barrel real hard, pressed up against my temple and I got to admit even in the dream I don't like the barrel pressed up against my temple, so I say something like, "Look man," or, "Shit, you know how it is sometimes, Steven," or, hell, even, "How was rehab?" you know, because I've always really, really rooted for the guy—even now, like today, waking up, having one of those "Steven's all fucked up on crack chasing me with a .357" dreams, even though she's fucking some other guy now, some older guy, some fat guy who looks nothing like me or (I hear) Steven and I'm not eating out of Steven's bowls anymore or watching TV from his chair or wiping my cock on his towel or (I'll admit) trying on his sports jackets sometimes when nobody's around, I still call Janelle and say, "Hey, babe, how's that Steven doin' anyway?"

"I don't know," she says, which makes me think she does, because when she really doesn't she always says all these things like, "I think he's sleeping under the bridge over there where the 101 crosses Alvarado because I drove by there the other night with the dogs and they started barking like crazy at some guy in the shadows and I called but no one came and I don't know—don't you think if it was a bum, he would've at least come?" or she says, "I'm afraid he's dead," but she doesn't say all that shit, she just says she doesn't know and her voice gets all quiet and then she tells me right out of nowhere—like I really want to know—that she's reading some book by D.H. Lawrence and I think: fuck, J, D.H. Lawrence?

Zan Nordlund

Upscale in Escondido

"Ain't no *Oak Hills* in Escondido, Mister Big Shot wit the fancy char... rri... o... t," cranked the old man. He spat on the ground. He was missing one full front tooth and half of the other and wearing only a pair of dirty khaki chinos and a white T-shirt. He had a soft pack of Kents rolled up in the left sleeve. I knew they were Kents because I could see the green of the package showing through the worn-out material. From the looks of him, they wouldn't last long.

Just then I heard the screen door of the mobile home behind me slam. The unmistakable screech of my ex-step mother sung like a rusty hinge. It stuck to the dewy haze of the late morning sun. Betty was barefoot and clad only in a shocking pink and aqua gauze skirt and a bright-white peasant top. She floated across her front lawn with all the melodrama of a star dancer in a sixth-grade production of *Swan Lake*. Her outfit revealed a generous amount of cleavage for a woman her age. Her beaded earrings dangled below the crest of her shoulders. Her toenails were painted a gaudy bright red. The polish was chipped. Her hair seemed to have been bleached one too many times. It looked as though it might be falling out. She sported a deep tan, unfortunate for the wrinkles around the corners of her eyes and mouth, and for those between her breasts. I wondered how she managed to walk wearing three toe rings on one foot.

"It's about time!" she hollered as she careened over to give me a hug. She'd been in California a long time—it'd taken its toll on her diction. She tried desperately now to muster all of the New England accent she could recall for my sake. It didn't work. "Well, I had to stop for gas. And to pee. It's a long drive," I said.

"Yes. Yes. It is. *Nice* car," she tittered as she shot a quick glance toward the wayward neighbor. He now unabashedly sat in a bright-blue plastic lawn chair between a pink flamingo and a rainbow-colored pinwheel on his front lawn so he could watch the show.

"It's a rental."

"Shhhh... let's go in and get out of the sun, shall we?" she said as she pushed me up a set of rusty metal stairs and into her trailer.

Some things never changed. There she was. Sixty-seven years old and still putting on airs for the neighbors, even if they were old drunks in a broken-down trailer park in the poorer section of Escondido. A familiar musty smell filled my nostrils. Every place she's ever lived has smelled this way...

According to her, it was all her fault.

Her children had succeeded in life because of her (she included me in this list of credits, although she hadn't given birth to me, or even laid eyes on me more than twice in over three decades). The fact that she had been a drunk, the fact that she had been neglectful, abusive, the fact that she'd done nothing to contribute to their education, either emotionally or financially, the fact that she had given me away before I'd reached the age of seven never daunted her. She still took credit. She was "Super Mom" and everybody better know it.

It was the hat that I remember the most. The big yellow hat. My grandmother showed up wearing a silky, flowered, yellow dress with matching gloves and a big yellow hat. I never saw anything like it. I was six at the time. My grandfather was shorter than she was and wearing a dark pair of pants and a plaid sports coat, tame by comparison. He smelled like Old Spice and cigars. I was afraid of them both. I knew they were going to change my life, though nobody ever told me anything.

At the end of the day, Betty came walking downstairs with my 'Get Smart' suitcase, the one with the full-color picture of Maxwell and Agent 99 on its side, packed with all of my worldly belongings in one hand and my teddy bear with the nose chewed off in the other. She handed them to Jack, my grandfather, and that was that. No tearful *good-bye*. No *I'm sorry, but we have to*. Nothing. Just a *See ya*. And that was that.

The other children in the family grew up to suffer. They lived through her alcoholism, her drug abuse, her sexual exploration, through her beating them with belts, neglecting them for her own needs, and through her multiple marriages to men younger than they were. They, in turn, had to live through their own multiple marriages, drug and alcohol problems, and difficulty in relating to their own children.

Thirty years later, there I was looking for her address on a well-worn piece of yellow Post-It paper I'd been carrying around in my wallet for two decades. She'd been begging me to come and visit "Before it was too late." It plainly said "Oak Hills."

The old man had said, "There ain't no Oak Hills in Escondido." I'd followed her directions *implicitly* and here I was.

Just like Betty, I thought, gazing out of the grimy picture window of her 1972 Champion Deluxe Special with original features.

Then I saw the justification for the title she'd bestowed upon her property. There, on the very edge of her corner lot, if one leaned slightly to the right, they could see an ever-so-very brief incline, and atop it rested a small Oak sapling.

I'm terribly sorry maam...
my name is Jesus pancakes.

Contributors

Adam Cole

Adam lives in San Francisco, CA, where he feigns dedication to many worthless activities, including blinking twice in a row and obligatory chuckling. One day, he hopes to commit to brushing twice daily, but will settle for vigorous flossing until said day arrives.

Alex Bosworth

Alex Bosworth was born in La Mesa, CA, on August 3, 1965. His influences are Franz Kafka, Mark Twain, and Kurt Vonnegut. He wanted to be a psychic but was afraid of what people might think.

Andrew Bomback

Andrew Bomback lives in North Carolina where he works as an internal medicine resident. His writing has appeared in *Pindeldyboz, Hobart, Crab Orchard Review, New York Stories, Diagram,* and also *Elysian Fields Quarterly.*

Anya Ezhevskaya

Current UCSD Religion/Linguistics undergrad with artistic, literary, and climbing tendencies. A passionate servant of Jesus Christ and an ammature poetry geek who hopes her work may in some way be encouraging to others. Otherwise, why bother? Her poem, "I Don't Speak English," now appears in her book *Twenty One and Counting* available at *booksurge.com.*

Beau Gunderson

Beau Gunderson suffers from Eighties Hair Rock Syndrome. The primary symptoms are a constant use of a red bandana, air-guitar at inappropriate times, a highly ritualized daily supplication to Guns N' Roses and/or Whitesnake videos, and an unhealthy obsession with guitar solos. Visit *fakepope.com* for more on Beau and his illnesses.

Blake Butler

Blake Butler lives in Georgia and is currently pursuing an MFA from Bennington College. He also edits a literary website called *Lamination Colony*. His work can be found at *deadwinter.com*.

Bob Surrat

Bob Surratt resides in Golden Hills with his fiancée, Zar, and small dog, Joey. Bob likes hip-hop and poetry. He is also a part-time student at San Diego City College and a full-time employee of the San Diego Public (Central) Library.

Cheryl Tupper

Catholic-Buddhist-Nerd-Goddess of Smoke, author of *Quantum Theory of Romance* and *Fluid Control Devices*, is currently working on the novel *Afterlife of Tamaki Jones*.

Daniel Touchet

Prone to doing the other thing, Daniel Touchet can often be found rendering various images in a fashion that rivals most anorexics' abilities to regurgitate undesirables. Things by Daniel at *itsajellyfish.com*.

Darby Larson

Darby Larson has had literature published online in many places. He's a staff writer for *Dicey Brown Magazine*. His favorite color is green. Visit his website at *darby.tv*.

David Barringer

David Barringer has published three fiction collections, designs book covers and posters for bands and lit journals, and sells his Dead Bug Funeral Kit on his website at *davidbarringer.com*. Word Riot Press will be publishing his first novel in the spring of 2005. Hopefully.

David Gianatasio

His work has appeared online or in print in *McSweeney's*, *Pindeldyboz*, *the Boston Globe*, *Quick Fiction*, *Eyeshot*, and elsewhere.

Dennis Mahagin

Dennis Mahagin's debut poetry collection, entitled *Grand Mal*, is forthcoming from *Suspect Thoughts Press*. Online, his work appears at *Absinthe Literary Review*, *42opus*, *3 A.M.*, *Stirring*, *Deep Cleveland*, and *Frigg Magazine*—among other publications..

Doug Tanoury

Doug Tanoury is primarily a poet of the Internet with the majority of his work never leaving electronic form. Make sure you visit his website at *home.comcast.net/~dtanoury1/Tanoury.html*.

Duane Locke

Duane lives in Lakeland, Florida, has had 5,295 poems published.

Emily Larlham

Emily Larlham went to Greece to save the turtles. She's back now.

Ian Thal

Ian Thal is a Boston-based poet, puppeteer, and mime artist. His poetry has appeared in *Tokens: Contemporary Poetry of the Subway*, *Flash!Point*, *Out of the Blue Writers Unite*, *Poesy*, and the 2003 Boston Cyberarts Festival. Ian also performs with both *Cosmic Spelunker Theater* and *Bread & Puppet Theatre*. Visit *authorsden.com/ianthal*.

Jackie Corley

Jackie Corley developed *Word Riot* (*wordriot.org*). Her writing has appeared at *SerialText* and *Little Engines* (*tnibooks.com*). She also personally maintains *crazyjackie.com*.

James Stegall

James is the author of *Retail Commando*, a collection of essays and short stories, and a novel, *The Brick*. He is a co-founder of *So New Media* (*sonewmedia.com*) and has written for numerous publications both online and off. He can be followed at *stegall.org*.

Jamie Allen

Jamie Allen is an Atlanta-based writer.

Jennifer Chung

Jennifer is an arts and entertainment writer, editor, and sometime-poet, based in San Diego. Born in Taiwan, she grew up embracing two cultures and strives to bring the often unheard female Asian-American voice to artistic, cultural, and political discourse.

Jennifer Lawson-Zepeda

Jennifer's poetry, prose, and essays have been featured in several literary magazines. Her work revolves around border issues and oppressive behaviors. Currently, she lives in Playas de Tijuana, Mexico with her husband, while her agent markets two novels on her behalf.

Jensen Whelan

Jensen Whelan's short fiction and poetry have appeared or are forthcoming with *Eyeshot, Surgery of Modern Warfare, Pindeldyboz, The Glut, Hobart, Ink Pot, NFG, Uber* and many others. He lives in Stockholm and maintains *journalofmodernpost.com*.

Jeremy Vaughan

mykungfugrip.com.

Jesse Eisenhower

underablanket.com.

Jimmy Jazz

Jimmy Jazz is.

Judd Hampton

Two time *Pushcart* Nominee, Judd lives in northern Alberta, Canada with his wife and two children. His fiction has appeared in *Night Train, Vestal Review, Paumanok Review, Danforth Review,* & *NFG*.

Karl Lintvedt

Karl Lintvedt is 24 and worships the sun. *karllintvedt.com.*

Kevin Fanning

Kevin Fanning lives in Illinois. He's currently working on a novel about being lost. Visit *whygodwhy.com*.

Lee Klein

Lee Klein edits *Eyeshot.net* and currently lives in Iowa City. "One, Two, What" was posted online by *The Konundrum Engine*. His first book is available from the publisher of the book you're holding at *temporaryworld.com*. Lots on Lee at *eyeshot.net/leeklein.html*.

Lisa McMann

Lisa McMann lives to write and writes to live. Her story, "The Day of the Shoes," won a 2004 Power of Purpose Award. She is nearly finished with her first novel *The Driftwood Letters of Cricket and Blue* and is working on a humorous non-fiction book called *Moving Across America: An Obsessive-Compulsive Journal*. Her published stories can be found on her website *lisamcmann.com*.

Liza Ezhevskaya

Liza believes we can know and be known, love and be loved.

Martha Ambrose

Martha has a BA in Graphic Design and is currently working on a teaching credential. She uses her time to contribute to independent magazines such as *the hall*, and volunteers at the San Diego Art Department for the Summer Youth Art Camp. Martha's current project can be observed at *luminal.cjb.net*.

Michael Fowler

Mike Fowler is one of those pasty-white, breathless fiction geeks who writes four bad short stories a month and then thinks he has to get each one of them posted or printed somewhere. It's sad.

Michael W. Graves

Michael Graves is the author of several books on computer technology. His latest, *The Complete Guide to Networking and Network+*, has been adopted as a textbook at several colleges and universities. When he's not writing or fixing somebody's computer, Mr. Graves is untangling his fly line from the branches overhead.

Michael Klam

Michael Klam coordinates poetry and art events for the Museum of the Living Artist in Balboa Park, San Diego (*sandiego-art.org*). His work has appeared in *Artecultura, Slipstream, Shiela Na Gig, Planeta, Jazz Shack Tea Bags* (*onecity.com/pirate/pe13/pe13.html*), *Jalons, Oikos, resistmuch.com*, and *lynnharper.com*. He won the 2002 San Diego Grand Slam, the La Paloma Invitational Slam, and the first day of the National Poetry Slam, 2002. His poem "Inner Flojo" appeared previously in his book *Sheep Go Mad* (collection, 2002).

Mike Coppolino

Coppolino is 35. Currently, he obsessively and compulsively designs religious objects with questionable value, works to complete his first novel, and acts as a consultant for wholesale bong distributors.

Neil Whitacre

Neil Whitacre grew up in Iowa and has lived in Milwaukee, Chicago, Miami, and The Everglades. He now resides in NY with Naomi Montgomery and their cat Jeff. He is obsessed with saltwater fishing and sea kayaking to the point where he can only allow himself to go a few times a year. His other interests include running and camping. He sounds like a real sissy, doesn't he? I mean he sounds like one of those asshole white dudes that would drive an Outback and wear all Patagonia gear and drink wine or something.

Paul A. Toth

Paul lives in Michigan. His novel *Fizz* is available from Bleak House Books. His short fiction has appeared or will soon appear in *Night Train, The Barcelona Review, Iowa Review Web, Mississippi Review Online,* and many others. See *netpt.tv*.

Ryan Kennebeck

This is the dream Ryan Kennebeck had one night: he died, turned all static red electricity, and saw dead electricity people walking around everywhere—blue, white, red—he asked one *What does this mean?* and the guy said *The color you are is the amount of hate you died with.* Ryan blinked, *I didn't think I had this much hate* and the guy shrugged, *It's not something you'd know about yourself.* He woke up feeling like he was falling. *How it Changed his Sense of Humor*, a story collection, will come out soon from Better Non Sequitur.

Savannah Schroll

A much shorter version of Savannah's "Famous" originally appeared on *insolentrudder.org* in December 2003. Her essays have appeared in the *European Journal of Cultural Studies* and *Modernism/Modernity*. She regularly reviews art and photography books for *Library Journal*. An illustrated collection of her short fiction called *The Famous & The Anonymous: The Deep & Darkly Secret* is now available from Better Non Sequitur. Find more of her world at *malaproductions.com*.

Scott Halligan

Scott Halligan is a classically-trained musician and beer connoisseur. He lives in a Volkswagen Vanagon in California.

Stephen Ausherman

Stephen Ausherman's latest book is a collection of travel stories titled *Restless Tribes* (Central Ave Press, 2004). He lives in New Mexico. For more info, visit *restlesstribes.com*.

Steve Delahoyde

Steve used to write a lot more than he does now. Currently, he works in post-production in Chicago, a city not unlike your own, except it's cooler and has a big lake. His collection of letters, "Nobody Appreciates my Talent," was previously published online by *Haypenny* (no longer in service). Find some of Steve's stuff at *ic.funk.nu/steve.html*.

Tom H. Macker

Tom lives in LA where he is more than likely working on something he calls *Ugly Girl/Pretty Girl*, versions of which have appeared at *Pindeldyboz.com*, *Monkeybicycle.net*, and *Facsimilation.com* (where "Things To Say About Books I Haven't Read" also once appeared).

Zan Nordlund

Zan served as a professor of English with Johnson & Wales University and as a member of a writer's consortium with Brown University. She is a Grand Prize winner of the *Chicken Soup for the Soul 10th Anniversary International Writer's Contest*. Her works have appeared in *The Back Bay Beacon*, *The Boston Globe*, *TimeLife Publications*, *Spillway Review*, *Moondance*, *Ken*Again*, *Dead Mule*, *Retrozine*, *a Journal of Memories*, and *Mipoesias*. Her first novel, *Altered Realty*, is under contract. Look for her on the web.

SUBMIT YOUR WORK

BOOM! For Real accepts submissions of prose, poetry, and pictures.

Email files to *submit@boomforreal.com*. Hard copies of artwork are also accepted. Send 'em to:

> BOOM! For Real
> P.O. Box 420303
> San Diego CA, 92142

Poetry & Prose: Please send files by electronic mail. Any file format is fine, but Word documents are very nice, especially when they include the author's name and title of work(s). These should be poems or short-short stories (approximately 1000 words or less). There are no other restrictions.

Pictures: Vector graphics, such as those created in Illustrator, are ideal! Black and white line-art too! (That means no gray, sorry.) Otherwise, one may also send either hard copies by molecular mail, or compressed JPEG or GIF files by email only if one has high-resolution (600 DPI) versions to be mailed later on CD before print. Artwork should be relatively small format to fit page dimensions of 5.5 x 8.5 inches. Images should stand alone on an otherwise white page. Submissions with backgrounds, gradation, and those which require a border are not acceptable. Sorry, no paintings or photography.

boomforreal.com

ABOUT THE PUBLISHER

Better Non Sequitur publishes books of towering quality.
betternonsequitur.com

SEE ALSO

How it Changed his Sense of Humor
by Ryan Kennebeck

A collection of short stories coming very soon.

The Famous and the Anonymous
by Savannah Schroll

Twenty-two tales that uncover the private obsessions and subterranean desires of the nameless and the internationally recognized.
darklysecret.com

Incidents of Egotourism in the Temporary World
by Lee Klein

A travelogue about finding the unexpected in familiar places.
temporaryworld.com

Sandwich
by Steven Coy

A collection of short stories, screenplays, and illustrations.
sandwich.betternonsequitur.com

Rubix Cube Dinner
starring Kürt Norby and Karla Saia

A laughable, half-hour (film) conversation between man and woman over their meals of Rubix Cubes.
rcd.betternonsequitur.com

THANK YOU!

Sammy Crutchinfieldson - San Diego, CA
Ian Whitacre - San Diego, CA
Brian & Tina Coy - San Diego, CA
Nick & Heidi Cascio - San Diego, CA
Jody Halligan - San Diego, CA
Mike Cascio - San Diego, CA
Joe & Karen Cascio - San Diego, CA
Donald Creekmore - Tempe, AZ
Jeff & Kathy Bruhn - San Diego, CA
Cindy Stevens - San Diego, CA
C. Fontane - San Diego, CA
John Hamilton - San Diego, CA
Beau Gunderson - Fall City, WA
Jeremy Watkins - San Diego, CA
Beth Alderete - Las Vegas, NM
Gary Carter - San Diego, CA
Jamie Allen - Kennesaw, GA
Jason DePasquale - Ann Arbor, MI
Daniel Touchet - San Diego, CA
Edgar Morales - San Diego, CA
John Swartz - Bronxville, NY
Michael Klam - San Diego, CA
Randy Murphy - San Diego, CA
Throop Roebling - Iowa City, IA
Savannah Schroll - Dover, PA